# NOTRE DAME vs. USC
## THE RIVALRY

## DON LECHMAN

THE
History
PRESS

Published by The History Press
Charleston, SC 29403
www.historypress.net

*Cover images, front top*: The Notre Dame–USC rivalry featured the Trojans' great running back Ricky Bell (left) and quarterback Pat Haden (right), while Notre Dame had quarterback George Izo and Coach Joe Kuharich (both center), who went 3-1 against USC.

First published 2012

ISBN 978.1.5402.2130.8

Library of Congress CIP data applied for.

*This book is dedicated to my two favorite Notre Dame and USC graduates: my late brother-in-law, Michael "We Are ND" Greeley, and Randy "Fight On!" Gray, a close friend since 1966.*

# CONTENTS

Acknowledgements                                                                7
Introduction                                                                    9

**PART I: THE GAMES**
Knute Rockne (4-1) vs. Howard Jones (1-4), 1926–1930                            13
Hunk Anderson (0-3) vs. Howard Jones (3-0), 1931–1933                           22
Elmer Layden (4-2-1) vs. Howard Jones (2-4-1), 1934–1940                        26
Frank Leahy (1-0) vs. Sam Barry (0-1), 1941                                     32
Frank Leahy (4-1-1) vs. Jeff Cravath (1-4-1), 1942–1950                         34
Frank Leahy (3-0) vs. Jess Hill (0-3), 1951–1953                                42
Terry Brennan (1-2) vs. Jess Hill (2-1), 1954–1956                              45
Terry Brennan (2-0) vs. Don Clark (0-2), 1957–1958                              48
Joe Kuharich (1-0) vs. Don Clark (0-1), 1959                                    49
Joe Kuharich (2-1) vs. John McKay (1-2), 1960–1962                              50
Hugh Devore (1-0) vs. John McKay (1-0), 1963                                    53
Ara Parseghian (3-6-2) vs. John McKay (6-3-2), 1964–1974                        55
Dan Devine (0-1) vs. John McKay (1-0), 1975                                     73
Dan Devine (1-4) vs. John Robinson (4-1), 1976–1980                             74
Gerry Faust (0-2) vs. John Robinson (2-0), 1981–1982                            81
Gerry Faust (3-0) vs. Ted Tollner (0-3), 1983–1985                              83
Lou Holtz (1-0) vs. Ted Tollner (0-1), 1986                                     85
Lou Holtz (6-0) vs. Larry Smith (0-6), 1987–1992                                87
Lou Holtz (3-1) vs. John Robinson (1-3), 1993–1996                              91
Bob Davie (0-1) vs. John Robinson (1-0), 1997                                   95
Bob Davie (2-1) vs. Paul Hackett (1-2), 1998–2000                               95

Bob Davie (1-0) vs. Pete Carroll (0-1), 2001     99
Tyrone Willingham (0-3) vs. Pete Carroll (3-0), 2002–2004     100
Charlie Weis (0-5) vs. Pete Carroll (5-0), 2005–2009     104
Brian Kelly (1-1) vs. Lane Kiffin (1-1), 2010–2011     108

**PART II: THE COACHES**
No. 1: Lou Holtz of Notre Dame (9-1-1), 1985–1996     112
No. 2: Pete Carroll of USC (8-1-1), 2001–2009     115
No. 3: Frank Leahy of Notre Dame (8-1-1), 1941–1953     119
No. 4: John Robinson of USC (8-3-1), 1976–1982, 1993–1997     122
No. 5: John McKay of USC (8-6-2), 1960–1975     125
No. 6: Howard Jones of USC (6-8-1), 1931–1940     127
No. 7: Knute Rockne (4-1), 1926–1930     129
No. 8: Elmer Layden (4-2-1), 1934–1940     131
No. 9: Joe Kuharich (3-1), 1959–1962     132
No. 10: Terry Brennan of Notre Dame (3-2), 1954–1958     134
No. 10: Gerry Faust of Notre Dame (3-2), 1981–1984     135
No. 10: Bob Davie (3-2), 1997–2001     135
No. 13: Ara Parseghian of Notre Dame (3-6-2), 1964–1974     136
No. 14: Jess Hill of USC (2-4), 1951–1956     139
No. 15: Hugh Devore of Notre Dame (1-0), 1963     140
No. 16: Lane Kiffin (1-1), 2010–2011     140
No. 16: Brian Kelly of Notre Dame (1-1), 2010–2011     141
No. 18: Paul Hackett (1-2), 1998–2000     142
No. 19: Dan Devine of Notre Dame (1-5), 1975–1980     143
No. 20: Jeff Cravath of USC (1-5-1), 1942–1950     144
No. 21: Sam Barry (0-1), 1941     145
No. 22: Don Clark of USC (0-3), 1957–1959     145
No. 22: Hunk Anderson of Notre Dame (0-3), 1931–1933     146
No. 22: Tyrone Willingham (0-3), 2002–2004     147
No. 25: Ted Tollner of USC (0-4), 1983–1986     147
No. 26. Charlie Weis of Notre Dame (0-5), 2005–2009     148
No. 27: Larry Smith of USC (0-6), 1987–1992     149

Appendix I: Heisman Trophy Winners     151
Appendix II: Fifty of Notre Dame's Greatest Players     153
Appendix III: Fifty of USC's Greatest Players     155
Bibliography     157
About the Author     159

# ACKNOWLEDGEMENTS

I would like to thank my wife, Patricia, and my daughter, Laura Ann, for putting up with my sporting obsessions. They seldom objected when I wanted to watch, listen to or attend any event having to do with a ball, but mainly football, basketball and baseball. They usually tagged along or watched with little complaint and a lot of enthusiasm. I would also like to thank my best friend, son David Michael, for his companionship in enjoying these events. He said they were some of the highlights of his childhood, and I treasure that sentiment and those moments, which are fortunately still being created today. Next, I would like to thank my commissioning editor, Jerry Roberts, for having the smarts, faith and courage to assign me a book that had to be completed in a very short time. It appears the task was not impossible. Also, I would like to express my profound admiration to Collegiate Collection, Notre Dame Archives and Sporting News Archives for their infinite wisdom in allowing the use of their images. In addition, the University of Notre Dame (ND) and the University of Southern California (USC) deserve kudos for providing eighty-five years of exciting football, which has helped make this infinitely exciting tome possible. Finally, I want to applaud all you people out there who have enjoyed the wonderful Irish-Trojan rivalry and wish to relive those golden moments once again—or even for the first time!

# INTRODUCTION

The oldest recorded rivalries in college Division I football are Army vs. Navy and Wisconsin vs. Minnesota, both of which started in 1890. The oldest rivalry among all schools is Yale vs. Princeton, which began in 1873. Every self-respecting football fan has to have a favorite rivalry. Mine growing up was Colorado vs. Nebraska (sadly no longer scheduled since the teams moved to different conferences). But there are still many heated rivalries among college's greatest teams. Every fan should have his own priority, but here are some of the longtime rivalries that have created the greatest national interest over the years—usually because they were battling for national ranking:

- MICHIGAN VS. OHIO STATE. Since they first played in 1897, the Wolverines hold a 57-41-6 edge over their hated rivals.
- OKLAHOMA VS. TEXAS. The Longhorns surprisingly own a 59-42-5 record over the Sooners since they first played in 1900.
- ALABAMA VS. AUBURN. The Crimson Tide leads in the series, 41-34-1. The rivalry started in 1893, but the series was often interrupted.
- ARMY VS. NAVY. Even though they are not usually among the national powers, their games create a lot of interest because of the national pride in our military. Navy leads the series, 56-49-7.
- COLORADO VS. NEBRASKA. Of course, I have to mention the Buffs and the Cornhuskers, even if it is not much of a rivalry. Hopefully, it will be resumed as a nonconference game. Huskers were leading, 48-19-2. Sad.

- MICHIGAN VS. MICHIGAN STATE. Their first game in 1898 was won by Michigan, 39–0. Nothing has changed much since then. The Wolverines lead, 67-32-5.
- STANFORD VS. CALIFORNIA. The Cardinals have dominated this great rivalry against the Golden Bears going back to 1892.

These are some of the big boys, but there are a lot of other teams with meaningful rivalries for their fans. Minnesota and Wisconsin (known as the game for Paul Bunyan's Axe) have battled 121 times since 1890, with the Gophers leading, 59-54-8. Missouri and Kansas (Border War) have tangled 120 times, with the Tigers holding a 56-55-9 edge. Texas and Texas A&M (Lonestar Showdown) have played 118 games, with the Longhorns unsurprisingly holding a 76-37-5 lead. Purdue and Indiana (Old Oaken Bucket) fought 114 times, with the Boilermakers on top, 71-37-6.

But it is doubtful that any rivalry in the history of college sports can equal the importance of Notre Dame/University of Southern California showdowns. The two powerhouses have met 83 times, with the Irish winning 43 to 35 for the Trojans, with 5 ties. USC has held the reign since 1996, going 12-4-1. Both teams have acted like a spoiler toward the other. In 1968, ND tied USC, 21–21, clouting them out of first place. It spoiled USC's undefeated season hopes by beating it in the last game of the season in 1947 and 1952. The Irish also gave the Trojans their first loss of the season in 1927, 1973 and 1995. Finally, the No. 1 Irish beat the No. 2 USC in 1988, 27–10, to ensure the national championship for ND. On the other hand, the Trojans have personally ruined Irish national championship hopes in 1980, 1971, 1970, 1964, 1938 and 1931.

Both teams have reveled in their glory as each has claimed eleven national championships. The Irish have also had seven Heisman Trophy winners (Angelo Bertelli, 1943; Johnny Lujack, 1947; Leon Hart, 1949; Johnny Lattner, 1953; Paul Hornung, 1956; John Huarte, 1964; and Tim Brown, 1988) compared to six for the Trojans (Mike Garrett, 1965; O.J. Simpson, 1968; Charles White, 1979; Marcus Allen, 1981; Carson Palmer, 2002; and Matt Leinert, 2004—Reggie Bush had to give his back in 2005). Notre Dame has won 845 games through 2011, while USC has 766 victories. Notre Dame has the poorer bowl record at 15-16, while USC is far superior at 31-16.

Notre Dame has seven of the greatest teams of all time (1924, 1929, 1946, 1947, 1966, 1973 and 1988), while USC is said to have five of the greatest teams of all time (1928, 1932, 1962, 1972 and 2003). USC had six last-minute wins against ND in 1931, 1964, 1978, 1996, 1997 and 2005, while the Irish had three last-minute victories in 1926, 1986 and 1999. Out of nine decades, USC has dominated four (1930s, 1960s, 1970s and the 2000s), while ND has dominated two (1920s and 1940s). As far as football graduation rates, Notre Dame has longed reigned in the high 90 percent bracket, while the Trojans have always lingered in the 50 and 60 percentages. Both teams, of course, have had other individual awards and too many all-Americans and even consensus all-Americans to mention.

The coaches have had their share of the limelight. For Notre Dame, Lou Holtz finished 9-1-1 against USC in addition to Leahy at 8-1-1, Knute Rockne at 4-1 and Elmer Layden at 4-2-1. For USC, Pete Carroll led all with an 8-1 record. John Robinson was 8-2-1, and John Mackay was 8-6-1. The great Howard Jones was 6-9-1. Irish coach Brian Kelly and USC coach Lane Kiffin each won a game while hoping for bluer skies ahead.

Notre Dame has had four so-called dynasties. Knute Rockne coached the Irish to a 105-12-5 record from 1919 to 1929 for a winning percentage of .881. From 1964 to 1978, Ara Parseghian and Dan Devine accumulated a record of 148-33-5 for .806. From 1941 to 1958, Frank Leahy and Terry Brennan went 119-29-3 for .795. And Lou Holtz went 100-30-2 for .765 from 1986 to 1996. USC traveled behind with four dynasties. Pete Carroll leads off with an 83-19 record for a .814 winning mark from 2001 to 2009. Howard Jones went .750 with 121-36-13 from 1928 to 1939. John McKay and John Robinson went 231-75-12 for .750 (1960–75 for McKay and 1976–82 and 1993–97 for Robby).

USC has dominated the rivalry since 1996, going 12-4-1. It wasn't too close. They have won games by scores of 44–13, 45–14, 41–10, 44–24, 38–0, 38–3 and 31–17. Roll over, Knute!

A look at the games, the coaches and the players will put the rivalry into perspective.

PART I

# THE GAMES

## KNUTE ROCKNE (4-1) VS. HOWARD JONES (1-4), 1926–1930

### December 4, 1926:
### ND 13–USC 12 (L.A. Coliseum), 74,378

There are many stories about how the great USC–Notre Dame rivalry was born. One has Knute Rockne's wife, Bonnie, and Marion Wilson, wife of USC athletic director Gwynne Wilson, credited with starting the famous series between Notre Dame and the University of Southern California. According to the story, USC, seeking some national acclaim, sent its athletic director, Wilson, and his wife to meet with Notre Dame officials when the team was playing at the University of Nebraska. Mrs. Wilson supposedly convinced Mrs. Rockne how pleasant a game in sunny California could be every other year compared to the icy Midwest. So Mrs. Rockne convinced Knute, who was reluctant to travel that far, that the series was a good idea.

Another version is promoted by Harry Grayson, a Scripps-Howard newspaper writer, according to Jerry Brondfield in *Knute Rockne*. Grayson said that he called Howard Jones and suggested that the series was a good idea, and when Jones balked, Grayson indicated that Jones was afraid of

Knute. Then he called Rock and told him the same story; soon both coaches proclaimed that they were never afraid of anyone in their lives. And the series was born, Grayson claimed.

Those both make good stories, but it is more likely that the series was created for financial and political reasons, according to Murray Sperber in *Shake Down the Thunder.* Both colleges saw the advantages of the series, and administrators from both schools created the cross-country rivalry. It didn't hurt that ND coach Knute Rockne and USC's Howard Jones were friends. They played against each other when Jones was the coach of the University of Iowa, and supposedly Knute helped Howard land the job at USC.

Rockne obviously dominated the series with Howard, winning four games to one, but the first game in 1926 promised to be memorable even before it started. USC, led by Jones, who was destined to be one of the greatest coaches in NCAA history, already boasted shutouts of 74, 61, 42 and 27 points, losing only to Stanford, 13–12. There was talk of a national title, and a season-ending conquest of the Irish wouldn't hurt anything. Rockne had won his first national championship in 1924, and Notre Dame already had seven shutouts to its credit for the season. The only mar—and it was a big one—was the previous week's loss to Carnegie Tech by the ridiculous score of 19–0. Rockne, who was not present at the loss, took a lot of the blame for putting the game on the shoulders of Hunk Anderson. Even great coaches of the day attended the 1926 contest: Pop Warner of Stanford, Bob Zuppke of Illinois and Jones's brother, Tad, who was the head man at Yale. The game created a lot of interest as Notre Dame was favored by 10 points, and tickets were $3.50 but supposedly went for $1.00 per yard—$40.00 for the 40-yard line.

According to Steve Bisheff and Loel Schrader in *Fight On!,* "The contest dwarfed any event previously held in Southern California, including Notre Dame's appearance in the 1925 Rose Bowl and anything staged by nearby Hollywood. Adding color to the occasion was the 'Thundering Herd' appellation hung on the 1924 USC team."

Rockne was his usual cagey self, downplaying his team. "If we could have ended the season a week ago, we would have been all right," he said in Cameron Applegate's *Notre Dame vs. USC: The Game Is On,* "but the boys are pretty well fagged out now, and we're just taking a chance. I don't know how the boys will hold up, but they'll try." Right.

Neither team was able to make much progress in the first quarter. Notre Dame's big play was a pass by quarterback Charles Riley for 15 yards to halfback Ray Dahman, while the Trojan big gains were by quarterback Mort Kaer returning a punt 20 yards and gaining 17 yards off tackle. The tide changed early in the second quarter, with Riley taking the team on a 75-yard march, himself scoring on a 16-yard run around left end. The big gainer was 27 yards by fullback Harry O'Boyle, taking the ball right through tackle Jesse Hibbs.

Then it was USC's turn. A 71-yard drive, spearheaded by Kaer, culminated with him going 1 yard off tackle for the score. Kaer zoomed 30 yards off tackle in the drive and then passed 38 yards to Al Behrendt. Notre Dame's Gene Edwards made a score-saving tackle on the 1-yard line. But the extra point by Bruce Taylor was blocked, and ND led, 7–6, at half.

The only real scoring opportunity in the third quarter came when USC's Morris Badgro caught a 40-yard pass but was ruled offside. A little later, Kaer's pass was intercepted to end the threat.

Things started to go the Trojans' way in the fourth quarter as Al Scheving blocked a ND kick. Then USC's Don Williams, a 165-pound quarterback, carried the ball nine straight times, culminating the drive with a 5-yard burst through the middle. The kick of Morley Drury, the "Noblest Trojan of them all," bounced off the upright, so USC had to settle for a 12–7 lead.

O'Boyle took the kickoff to the 25-yard line, and then Riley completed a 28-yard pass to John Niemiec. But Riley's next pass was intercepted by Manuel Laraneta to end the threat. USC's Howard Elliott carried a punt to the 40-yard line but fumbled, and Notre Dame recovered. What happened next can only be described as surreal—or the greatest football coach in college going to work. Rockne called on little-used 145-pound halfback Art Parisien to go in for the great veteran Riley. People were awestruck. Many thought Rock had lost his marbles. Parisien was even a last-minute decision to make the trip. The little quarterback was practically squashed by a ton of Northwestern players a few weeks earlier and was carried from the field with what was diagnosed as a "bruised heart." It was said that doctors advised Rockne not to play him, but he allowed him to go on the trip.

Parisien had only one chance. He had to march the team down the field and score or he would be removed. The little lefthander, utilizing a hidden ball trick, gained 4 yards through the middle of the line. Then he threw to Niemiec for 25 yards to the USC's 20-yard line. Two quick-hitters through the line went nowhere. Frank Hogan went in for Fred Miller at left tackle, while John Fredericks took over for Bud Boeringer, an all-American, at center. People thought Rock had lost more marbles.

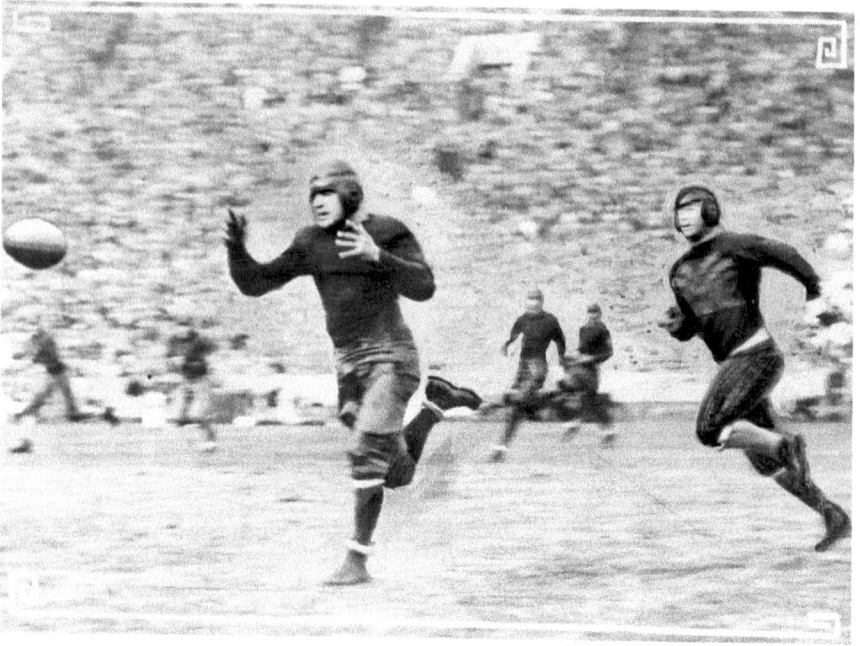

The first game in the Notre Dame–USC rivalry took place in 1926 at the Los Angeles Coliseum, with the Irish prevailing, 13–12. Reserve quarterback Art Parisien came off the bench to lead ND to victory. *ND Archives.*

Parisien took the snap and ran to his left, and when USC players converged to smother him, he threw a strike to the wide-open Niemiec, who cruised in from the 5-yard line. Jeff Cravath blocked the extra point, but it mattered little. Parisien was replaced after the kickoff by Vince McNally, who promptly intercepted a pass to end USC's last chance. Game over: ND 13–USC 12.

The teams were remarkably even. Where the Irish relied on passing and misdirection, USC was all power up the middle. Notre Dame had 162 yards from scrimmage and USC 132. However, 132 of the Irish yards came in the air, while the Trojans only had 39.

In the locker room after the game, Jones congratulated Rock and said, "Well, we almost did it. Congratulations, Knute."

"Thanks," Rockne said. "It was the greatest game I ever saw."

USC lost, but it obviously showed it could play with the big boys  It was only the start of spectacular things to come.

# The Games

## November 26, 1927:
## ND 7–USC 6 (Soldier Field, Chicago), 120,000

The year 1927 was just a prelude to USC's national championship in 1928, and this game was even bigger than the one the previous year. USC had won all of its games, except it tied Stanford and then lost to Notre Dame, costing them the national championship. Notre Dame was already out of the running because of a tie with Minnesota and an 8–0 pasting by Army.

But everyone was equally awaiting this game, as seen by the more than 120,000 at Soldier Field in Chicago. USC was ready, and Coach Jones predicted an offensive battle since USC was averaging forty-four points per game. Obviously, Notre Dame was not reading the same clippings.

"They were always tough," USC great Morley Drury said of the Fighting Irish, "because you had to play them hard for the full 60 minutes. You could never let down against Notre Dame."

For one thing, USC fans were leery because Notre Dame's great halfback and hero of last year's game, Butch Niemiec, was not supposed to play. Rockne said that "he wouldn't get into the game but would be suited up on the sidelines." No one, however, trusted Rock—the picture of integrity off the field but a man known to use a little guile on it. USC's roster, although unknown to most football fans today, featured a reserve lineman by the name of Marion Morrison. He was later known in movies as John Wayne.

The *Chicago Tribune* was amazed by the huge crowd. "Not all the boxes were occupied by notables and society folk, for the gangsters and detectives called off their shootings until after the game," it noted. "They were out in almost full force except a few, who didn't have tickets and were left in jail, but all the 'big shot hoodlums' were there, behaving just like gentlemen."

But the game was far from an offensive show. All the scoring was done in the first half, with a missed extra point by the Trojans being the deciding margin of victory. A typical Rockne moment took place at halftime, according to Sperber in *Shake Down the Thunder*, when he had some of the student body present a satirical skit making fun of "effete easterners who were trying to change the game of football from a he-man's sport into a silk-stocking contest," Sperber reported. Columnist Arch Ward noted that Rockne's speeches "became almost as famous as his gridiron exploits." Audiences "loved his appeal for he-men and his denigration of anyone less masculine," Sperber wrote.

After Notre Dame received the kickoff and was unable to advance the ball, John Elder punted short, and the Trojans took over on their own 40-

yard line. Drury led the Trojans to the Notre Dame 8-yard line. The Irish defense toughened, but on fourth down, Drury threw a touchdown pass to wide-open Russ Saunders. However, a faulty snap from center cost them an extra point—again. Now it was Notre Dame's turn. USC held ND, but a penalty on the punt—illegal use of hands—cost USC 15 yards and gave the Irish the ball on their own 49. But USC held, and eventually, after an exchange of punts, the Irish ended up with the ball on their own 46. The running of Christie Flanagan and Frank Collins moved them to the USC 27. After a few failed plays, quarterback Charles Riley delivered a TD pass to Ray Dahman, who also kicked the extra point, and Notre Dame led, 7–6.

That was all the scoring, as both teams stiffened in the second half. In the third period, USC was driving for a score when Riley, playing a defensive back, intercepted Drury's pass on his own 3-yard line. He took off until he was met in a jolting collision by Russ Saunders. The ball flew into the end zone, where USC recovered it—safety! Two points and the lead, 8–7. But no! Referee John Schommer called the play an incomplete pass, giving Notre Dame possession on its own 20-yard line.

It was a strange call. Even the heavily favored Note Dame crowd booed. Everyone thought it was obvious that the pass was complete. Even Schommer, when he looked at game film later, said, "It looks like I pulled a boner." But it was too late. The call stood. Neither team advanced much after that. Punter Dahman averaged about 44 yards per kick and Jesse Hibbs 49 for the Trojans. It was one of the great games in the historic rivalry—settled, unfortunately, by a disputed call.

"Bob Zuppke, famed Illinois coach, a spectator at the game, said at the time that the decision was a bad one," sportswriter Braven Dyer reported in the *Los Angeles Times*. "Other critics agreed, but, of course, the score stood. It all added color to the series." And the game was very lucrative, netting the Irish $123,909.

## December 1, 1928:
## USC 27–ND 14 (L.A. Coliseum), 72,632

Revenge was sweet in 1928 for USC as the Trojans and Notre Dame started a five-year reign of supremacy by the two schools not equaled in college sports. USC won the national championship in 1928, 1931 and 1932, and Notre Dame won in 1929 and 1930. When the two foes played their third game in 1928 at the Coliseum, USC was definitely in the driver's seat. The year 1928 marked the first (and only) time Rockne lost as many as three games—to Wisconsin, Georgia Tech and Carnegie Tech. Meanwhile, USC's only blemish was a 0–0 tie with California.

The West Coast fans were clamoring to see the USC powerhouse, so tickets were hard to come by—even if it was not sold out. Rockne received many special requests, reported Sperber in *Shake Down the Thunder*, and one was from ND alum Joe Gargan, who was the brother-in-law of Joseph P. Kennedy, the future president's father. When no money was forthcoming, Rock returned the tickets to the box office and sent this reply: "Gargan promised to send money for these boxes which has never been received. He must quit being a sponger and pay his way through the world."

"It should also be noted," said Bisheff and Schrader in *Fight On!*, "that Rockne sustaining four losses for the first time in his coaching career, converted to Catholicism during the off-season. Clearly, this was a man who covered all the angles"—or was that *angels*?

Oh yeah, and then there was the game. Quarterback Don Williams, end Lowry McCaslin, halfback Harry Edelson and fullback Russ Saunders helped put USC ahead, 20–0, at halftime. The big play in the second quarter was provided by USC defensive end Tony Steponovich. He blocked a pass from Butch Niemiec, managed to pick it off his shoe tops and rambled 18 yards for the touchdown.

Notre Dame rallied in the second half but not enough. Scoring first was halfback Jack Chevigny, who raced 51 yards up the middle for a touchdown thanks to great blocks from Frank Leahy (the future coach) and Fred Miller. Notre Dame scored once more, but so did USC, on another Williams to McCaslin pass, so the final ended up 27–14 for USC. USC allowed only 59 points the entire season, and in the following week, it was rewarded its first national championship.

"Southern California all but hugged the life out of the South Bend Irish," the *Los Angeles Times* reported, "and made it harder than ever for the folks back over the Great Divide to forget Los Angeles…The tang of the sea land the heart of the desert do not make sissies."

## November 16, 1929:
## ND 13–USC 12 (Soldier Field) 112,912

USC's euphoria was short-lived, as the Irish turned the tables on it in 1929, and Rock won his second national championship, finishing 9–0, allowing a total of 38 points the entire year. USC, meanwhile, lost only two games, but unfortunately, one was to Notre Dame. The Trojans won their first five games by a total of 216–7 and looked like they were on their way to another national championship. But first California got in the way, winning 15–7.

Meanwhile, Rockne himself was not having a great year medically. Phlebitis bothered him once again, but he was on the sidelines in a wheelchair for the USC game, even though his assistants ran the show—for a while.

USC got off to a fast start before 112,912 at Soldier Field. After the Trojans held Notre Dame on the opening drive, they took over on their own 48-yard line. After some gains by fullback Don Moses, quarterback Marshall Duffield passed to halfback Marger Aspit, who went 25 yards to score. The USC fans were aghast as, once more, the Trojans missed the extra point. In the second quarter, Notre Dame came back after quarterback Frank Carideo returned a punt to his own 46-yard line. After some setbacks, halfback Jon Elder passed 55 yards to the USC 10-yard line, where Captain Tom Conley caught the ball and sailed in for the score. This time, Carideo missed the extra point, making it 6–6 at halftime. But Rockne had had enough. He went to the locker room in his wheelchair at halftime.

"'Boys,' he started, his voice only an echo of its usual high pitched whine," reported Applegate in his book. "'Get out there and play them hard the first five minutes. They'll hate it, but play them hard. Remember, I'll be upstairs, but I'll be watching you. Go ahead now and hit 'em hard. Win. Win. Win' he shouted. 'That's the only reason for playing…crack 'em, CRACK 'EM. I'll be watching.'"

Applegate continued: "The doors of the dressing room shot open and not a man looked right or left as the fighting Irish took the field. Six minutes later fullback Joe Savoldi plunged over the USC goal line for 6 points. Carideo's extra point was good and Notre Dame led 13–6. The Rockne oratorical magic was still there."

But the game was not over. Notre Dame kicked to the 4-yard line, but Russ Saunders took the ball and rumbled 96 yards for a score. USC was back! But wait a minute. Lady luck struck again. This time, Don Musick missed the extra point, and the Irish won, 13–12. Failure to make extra points had cost USC a third game.

When the season ended, Applegate reported that Curly Lambeau, the first Green Bay Packer coach, asked the Rock what kind of team he had.

"The best damn team I ever had," Rockne said. "But I can't tell them that."
"Why?"

"They might believe me." It didn't matter. Rock's second national championship was in his pocket.

## December 8, 1930:
## ND 27–USC 0 (L.A. Coliseum), 73,967

The third and last championship was not far away. Before this game, Pop Warner had called USC one of the greatest teams of all time. It went into the Notre Dame game with five shutouts and only one loss, 7–6 to Washington State.

Meanwhile, Notre Dame was going to have to play without its outstanding fullback, Joe Savoldi, called the greatest running back since George Gipp. Joe had the temerity to get married as a freshman and get divorced as a sophomore. The good fathers sent him on his way.

"Rockne used great psychology with all the newspaper men," USC tackle Ernie Smith recalled in Ken Rappoport's book *The Trojans*. "He told them that he had nothing with [Joe] Savoldi out of the lineup...Well, we believed what we read in the newspapers, and here comes this Bucky O'Connor. We never get did get over that Notre Dame loss." Los Angeles writers made the Trojans as much as a four-touchdown favorite.

"I'm afraid we're going to take an awful beating from Southern California," Rockne said, according to Applegate, "but I'm willing to bet we won't be defeated by any four touchdowns, as some Los Angeles writers seem to feel. I do think, though, we'll be lucky to hold SC to a two-touchdown victory."

Rockne was not done yet. USC had actually invited him to address its team at a pregame banquet. "He explained his team's weaknesses and elaborated on their injuries, all the while praising the USC team as one of the finest he had ever seen," Applegate wrote. "When the game is over tomorrow," he said, "and I know you'll do everything to hold down the score...I'd like to ask you fine young men to come over and congratulate my boys on a fine game. It will mean so much to them to have a firm handshake and a kind word from a team like yours." They fell for it hook, line and sinker.

"The Irish of Notre Dame methodically dissected the best football team USC had fielded in years. Their line outrushed the Trojan forwards, their backs outran the Trojan backs, and the SC tacklers fell before the Notre Dame blockers like petals in a chill winter wind," Applegate noted.

Notre Dame started off by moving to the USC 20-yard line but turned the ball over on downs. USC promptly fumbled, and halfback Marchy Schwartz passed to quarterback Carideo for six. Carideo converted, and the score was 7–0. When Notre Dame got the ball back after an exchange of punts, halfback Marty Brill pitched to Bucky O'Connor, who skirted around right end for 80 yards and a touchdown. Then Dan Hanley caught a touchdown pass from Nick Lukats, but it was called back because of penalty. USC trailed at the half, 13–0.

The second half was more of the same. In the third quarter, Schwartz passed to O'Connor for another ND touchdown. Lukats then scored, making the final score 27–0. Notre Dame had won nineteen games in a row and its second consecutive national championship.

No one seemed to know what to expect from Rockne next. But it didn't matter. Four months later, on March 31, 1931, Knute Rockne was killed in a plane crash in a Kansas cornfield on his way to Los Angeles to help out with a movie, *The Spirit of Notre Dame*. The country lost a great character and a great coach but most of all a great man.

# HUNK ANDERSON (0-3) VS. HOWARD JONES (3-0), 1931–1933

## November 21, 1931:
## USC 16–ND 14 (Notre Dame), 50,731

Knute Rockne was gone, but Notre Dame didn't slow down in 1931 until the team met the Trojans. Jones dominated this series, with a Rock disciple, Hunk Anderson, winning all three.

"Notre Dame is so good that Hunk Anderson could lick any team he has played—Northwestern excepted—with his second string," USC scout Aubrey Devine told reporters upon returning from a scouting mission of the Fighting Irish in Rappoport's *The Trojans*. "It is impossible to set a fool-proof defense for the Irish because they are such a versatile squad. Just when you think you have them stopped, they break out in another direction."

"[We have] every reason to believe that the team we buck up against Saturday is much stronger than the one which trounced us 27 0 last year," Jones said. "On the other hand, there is nothing to indicate that my boys are any better than they were that day Knute Rockne's eleven made us look so bad."

Possibly USC's greatest win ever came in 1931 at ND Stadium when the Trojans, down 14–0 after three quarters, scored 16 points in the final period. The victory propelled the Trojans to their third national championship in four years. *ND Archives.*

So much for prognosticating. The Trojans started big. They went to the Irish 1-yard line after the kickoff only to have fullback Jim Musick fumble and Notre Dame recover. After an exchange, Notre Dame took over on its own 45 and, led by Marchy Schwartz and fullback Steve Banas, drove to a touchdown and a 7–0 lead at half. In the third quarter, Schwartz scored from the 10-yard line, and Charlie Jaskwhich kicked the extra point.

After Notre Dame took a 14–0 lead, *Los Angeles Times* columnist Braven Dyer wrote, "The score looked as big as the population of China. In fact it looked a darn sight larger than that, if possible, because of the consummate ease with which the Irish scored. The fury of Troy's attack in the second half astounded everybody."

After USC fullback Jim Musick broke his nose, Orv Mohler replaced Gus Shaver at quarterback, and Shaver took over for Musick. They eventually drove down to the one, and Shaver scored. Johnny Baker's extra point attempt was blocked—again. After the kickoff, the Irish failed to advance, and the Trojans got the ball back and drove into Irish territory. Shaver took it in for the score. Baker kicked the extra point, and ND still led, 14–13.

The Trojans got the ball back with three minutes to play. The Irish couldn't stop them. Shaver threw a 50-yard pass, and Ray Sparling made a great catch. But then the Irish defense rallied. Everyone suspected a pass play, but Mohler called for a field goal. "Baker and I have been practicing that play all year. I knew if it failed, I'd be the goat, and we would be licked, but old Bake doesn't miss on those short ones. I knew he wouldn't fail me. Wasn't it a beaut?"

"It did not seem humanly possible for them [USC] to win," Dyer wrote. But thanks to the indomitable fight of a great gang of kids...the Trojans achieved the greatest athletic triumph in Southern California history." USC came home to 300,000 strong cheering its victory. USC closed its season with three straight wins and Jones's third national championship.

## December 10, 1932:
## USC 13–ND 0 (L.A. Coliseum), 93,924

The Irish were 7-1 going into a game against USC—also in good shape having won eight games in a row, six by shutout. All-Americans guard Aaron Rosenberg and tackle Ernie Smith led a devastating defense.

"The 1932 team was the strongest defensive team that USC has ever had," said USC publicist Al Wesson in *USC Trojans*. "There was only two touchdowns scored on us all season—and they were both by passes. No one could move, no less score on the ground against us. Smith was one of the greatest tackles we ever had. Rosenberg was a smart, fine athlete. You could not buy a yard against this team. I'd say without question the offense of the 1931 team and the defense of 1932 were the best Jones produced." The year 1932 also marked the beginning of the career of the great Cotton Warburton, who was only a sophomore.

Notre Dame, meanwhile, was also having a great year. It shut out six opponents, with only a loss to Pittsburgh marring its record. The Irish boasted the great Moose Krause at left tackle, Steve Banas at fullback, Nick Lukats at left half and Harry Wunsch at right guard. But this game was no contest. The Trojans dominated the Irish in every aspect of the game. Led by quarterback Homer Griffith and Warburton, the Trojans scored a touchdown in each half to go away with a 13–0 victory before a 93,924 at the Coliseum.

# The Games

## November 25, 1933:
## USC 19–ND 0 (Notre Dame), 25,037

USC and Howard Jones continued their domination of the Irish with a 19–0 win in South Bend for their third straight win over Notre Dame, two by shutouts. Nothing much happened in the first quarter, but all-American Warburton took over in the second. Warburton, who became a very successful and honored film editor in Hollywood (he won an Academy Award for editing *Mary Poppins* in 1964) was almost impossible to stop in the second quarter. "After that," Applegate wrote, "They [the Irish] needed more than strength. They needed a net. Or a shotgun. Birdshot would have done. Cotton weighed 147...and he was speedy as a roadrunner and slippery as an eel. The Irish didn't land a hand on him all day."

The first quarter featured a 61-yard march; with Rosenberg opening holes and fullback Haskell Wotkyns helping Cotton, they moved to the end zone. The highlight was Cotton's 35-yard run, capped by his plunge for a touchdown.

Passing was the name of the game in the third quarter, when quarterback Bob McNeish threw the ball to Homer Griffith, who took it in for the TD. In the last quarter, the Irish's Andy Pilney tried a long pass to Johnny Young, but Cal Clemens intercepted and took it to the 29-yard line. After several runs, including

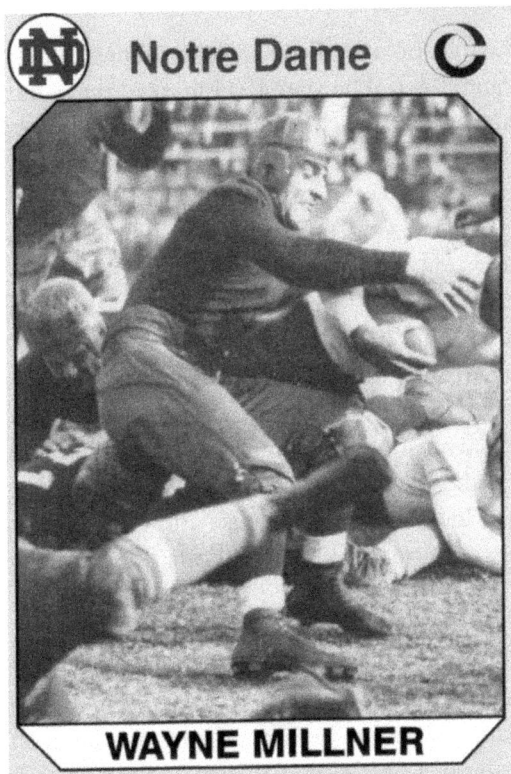

Wayne Millner was an all-American end for Notre Dame from 1933 to 1935. His record against USC was 2-1. *Collegiate Collection.*

three by Warburton, Cotton took it over for the final score. USC did not win another championship that year, but it finished 10-1-1.

And Notre Dame? "No university in the world is more win oriented than the University of Notre Dame," Applegate wrote. "They do not expect to lose, and they don't put up with it for long. That year, they lost five, won three and tied 1, their first losing season since 1887. It was Hunk Anderson's worst year...and his last."

# ELMER LAYDEN (4-2-1) VS. HOWARD JONES (2-4-1), 1934–1940

## December 8, 1934:
## ND 14–USC 0 (L.A. Coliseum), 45,568

After Howard wore out Hunk, he took on one of the Four Horsemen, Elmer Layden, with far less success, going 2-4-1. The year 1934 marked the debut of Layden, who served seven years as head coach and only lost 4 more games than Hunk. He also finished 4-2-1 against USC and 47-13-3 for his career.

As the game between USC and Notre Dame approached, the Irish looked to be in better shape than the Trojans, and they proved it. They had an all-American center in Jack Robinson, halfback George Melinkovich was returning after an injury and the backfield included Bill Shakespeare and Mike Layden, Elmer's little brother. They had only won five games, but USC only won four, and USC's two starting ends, Ward Browning and Leavitt Thurlow, both had broken legs.

"I don't know what we can do against Notre Dame," Howard Jones said in *Notre Dame vs. USC.* "Some of the boys played very badly last Saturday. Those who look good on defense, look terrible on offense and vice versa. It is too late to do much changing, and even if I could, I don't know exactly what it would be."

USC did stop Notre Dame on its first offensive thrust, recovered a fumble and tried for a field goal (that missed). That set the tone for the day. After several exchanges, Shakespeare threw a touchdown pass to Layden, and Wally Fromhart kicked the extra point. In the second period, the Irish scored again after Shakespeare threw a pass to end Wayne Millner. Cotton

Warburton knocked it away, but Millner caught it before it hit the ground—first down on the 2-yard line. Layden scored from the two, making it 14–0.

Applegate pointed out that USC actually played a very tough game. Haskell Wotkyins pounded the middle of the Irish line, and Warburton was great on defense. "Warren Hull was a workhorse at tackle," Applegate reported. "Alongside of him at right guard, Joe Preininger subbing for injured Bob Sanders, performed nobly...as did Gil Kuhn, Cal Clemens and three graduating seniors, Captain Julius Bescos, Herb Tatsch and Hueston Harper." The entire Trojan line played excellent football, but Notre Dame was just too much for them on that day.

Standing out for the Irish were Millner, Captain Dominic Vairo and tackle Joe Sullivan. Even Elmer Layden contributed in his best Rockne fashion, according to Applegate: "'We will be lucky to stay in that football game,' he cried. Even the press bought the story The *Los Angeles Times* said, 'The Cripples Arrive in Tucson.' 'You boys sure have that right,' said Layden. 'Even our train is limping.' Rockne would have been proud."

## November 23, 1935:
## ND 20–USC 13 (Notre Dame), 38,305

Notre Dame went into the 1935 game with 6-1-1 record, while USC had just won 1 after losing 4 in a row. Notre Dame was decent, but nobody expected much of a game, as only about thirty-eight thousand showed up at Notre Dame Stadium. The Trojans jumped off to a quick lead when Irish fullback Don Elser fumbled right after the start of the game, and Trojan fullback Cliff Propst recovered. Three plays later, quarterback Dave Davis scored from the six. The extra point attempt was blocked, and USC led, 6–0. Two more fumbles by the Trojans kept the score there at half.

Recalled halfback Nick Pappas in *The Trojans*:

*We were leading at the half, and we came back on the field after intermission...They're undefeated...We're holding on, and we're ahead and we walk on the field and they have a band covering the entire field waiting for us, and they strike up "Ave Maria" in the memory of Knute Rockne. So we all stand at attention, and they play it through twice. It was 18 degrees at South Bend...and it was soooo cold. In the meantime, the Notre Dame team is huddling underneath a blanket. Well, they finally kick off to us, one of our guys fumbles the ball at the 3-yard line, and they pick it up...and go in for a score. The damn band beat us.*

Notre Dame did turn things around quickly in the third quarter thanks to quarterback Wally Fromhart, playing his final game. First, Wally caught a 40-yard pass from quarterback Bill Shakespeare. Then he threw a 53-yard pass to Wayne Millner. To polish things off, he kicked both extra points.

But USC came right back. Quarterback Glenn Thompson threw a 24-yard pass to end Chuck Williams to the ND 3-yard line. Thompson scored from there, and Homer Beatty kicked the extra point to make the score 14–13.

Nobody was going to forget Fromhart's last game. He intercepted a Thompson pass on his own 10-yard line and galloped 82 yards to the Trojan 8. Bill Shakespeare went around end on the next play to score, and the final tally was 20–13. Notre Dame finished a decent 7-1-1, while the Trojans suffered at 5-7.

## December 5, 1936:
## ND, 13–USC 13 (L.A. Coliseum), 71,201

Having lost its last two games, USC went into this game as a decided underdog. Meanwhile, the Irish had only lost to two tough teams—Pittsburgh and Navy—and were favored by 20 points. It didn't take long for Notre Dame to score. Bob Wilke carried for 31 yards and threw a 40-yard pass to the other halfback, Nevin McCormack, and all of a sudden they were on the 3-yard line. Wilke took the ball over for the score, and the Irish led, 6–0. Right end Jim Henderson blocked Andrew Puplis's conversion attempt, and the score remained 6–0.

A whole new team came in the second quarter for the Irish. The backfield was led by quarterback Joe Ruetz and included Vic Wojchihovski, Jack McCarthy and Steve Miller. However, Gil Kuhn intercepted a pass at the Trojan 15 and took it back to the USC 25. Quarterback Ambrose Schindler rambled through the line for 11 yards when he either fumbled or lateraled— no one was sure—the ball to Dick Berryman, who rambled 65 yards for a touchdown. The extra point was missed by Henderson, and the score was tied.

Late in the second quarter, the Irish rolled again. They had a first down on the 9-yard line when a pass from Wilke was intercepted by Bud Langley at the 4-yard line. He was plodding down the field when he was cornered by ND fullback Larry Danbom with no way to escape. Here's Applegate's account of what happened next: "Help sometimes comes at the most unexpected times from the most unexpected sources. In this case it came

28

from Tom Louttit, and he wasn't even on the USC roster. He was a referee." Apparently, Louttit inadvertently got in Danbom's way all the way downfield, allowing Langley to score. This time Henderson kicked the extra point, and USC led, 13–6, at the half.

But in the second half, the Irish finally unleashed a devastating attack led by Wilke's passing and running. They moved down to the Trojans' 15, where Wilke threw a pass to Nevin McCormick for the touchdown. Puplis added the extra point, and the final was a 13–13 tie, the first time in the ten-year history of the series. Both teams threw passes all over the field in the fourth quarter, but to no avail. Puplis also tried a 25-yard field goal for the Irish, but left end Gene Hibbs blocked it.

It was kind of an embarrassing tie for the Trojans, but they took it. "We were lucky," Jones said. True. The Irish outgained the Trojans, 406 to 53. The Irish had thirteen first downs to zero for the Trojans. In fact, a punt hit a Trojan on the foot and was recovered by a Notre Dame player in the end zone. But the referee didn't see it hit the player and ruled it a touchback. The Trojans thought it was justice because of John Schommer's erroneous call in the 1927 game.

Classy Elmer Layden never offered excuses: "It was quite a ballgame... sometimes the breaks go your way, and sometimes they don't."

## November 27, 1937:
## ND 13–USC 6 (Notre Dame), 28,920

Things were getting tough for Howard Jones since USC had not beaten Notre Dame since 1933, and 1937 was no better. Notre Dame came into the game ranked ninth in the country with a 5-2-1 record, while the Trojans were a mediocre 3-3-2. USC was also missing four starters, and only about twenty-nine thousand showed up in Notre Dame Stadium during the heart of the depression. USC, however, was determined to beat its two biggest rivals—ND and UCLA—in the last games of the season.

USC dominated the first half thanks to one player, Grenville Lansdell, the backup for the injured Ambrose Schindler. He ran, passed and punted, taking the Trojans down to the Irish 9. After a 2-yard gain, Lansdell threw a pass to Gene Hibbs on the left side for the touchdown. That extra point bugaboo hit again, as Bob Holzman missed the kick. They took that lead into halftime but unfortunately never scored again. Notre Dame stopped a Trojan drive on their own 20 and then took off. Fullback Mario Tonelli crushed through the Trojan line and sprinted to the USC 13-yard line before being downed by halfback Owen Hansen. But Tonelli finished the drive, taking it in for the TD. The conversion made the final score 13–6. USC salvaged a poor season by beating UCLA, 19–13, the following week.

## December 3, 1938:
## USC 13–ND 0 (L.A. Coliseum), 97,146

At last! Salvation for Coach Jones—before about ninety-seven thousand no less. This was a sad day for the Irish and a great one for USC. Notre Dame was unbeaten (8-0) and heading for another national championship. Meanwhile, USC blew its chances by losing to Alabama in the first game of the season and then to Washington. Notre Dame had only allowed 39 points, but its offense lacked speed. Then star halfback Ben Sheridan was injured, and things did not look great, especially with USC coming off a 42–7 victory over UCLA.

The first quarter was even, but things started to happen after USC missed a 25-yard field goal. ND quarterback Bob Saggau was punting with fourth down and 22 yards to go when he decided to run with the ball. However, he fell short, and the Trojans took over. Later, when Layden was questioned about the decision, he replied, "A Notre Dame quarterback is always right, and that is that."

Regardless, the Trojans took over the ball on the Irish 39. Quarterback Ollie Day come in and did his stuff. First, he ran for 9 yards, and then he threw a 48-yard pass to Al Krueger, and USC led, 6–0, at half. In the third period, Notre Dame could do nothing.

In the fourth quarter, Notre Dame's Milt Piepul fumbled, and right half Jimmy Jones recovered on the Irish 35. Mickey Anderson's passing and Jack Banta's running moved them down to the three, where Bill Anderson crashed through for the score. Phil Gaspar kicked the extra point, and surprisingly, USC led, 13–0.

"We have no excuses," Coach Layden said later. "Our boys did not play their best game by a long shot, but we lost to a fine team."

# The Games

## November 25, 1939:
## USC 20–ND 12 (Notre Dame), 54,799

Shades of 1938! Notre Dame came into the USC game 7-1, having lost only to Iowa, 7–6. USC, meanwhile, had won five games and tied 1.

Coach Layden was fearful, saying, "This team potentially has the most versatile offense of any eleven in the country."

Jones said, "The cold and snow will just make our job more difficult."

Guard Harry Smith, tackle Phil Gaspar and guard Ben Sohn halted the Irish offense. Meanwhile, USC took over on its own 33 and went to the Irish 2-yard line in ten plays. Grenny Lansdell scored the touchdown, and true to form, Bob Robertson missed the extra point. Late in the second quarter, USC went to the ND 2-yard line, but Doyle Nave fumbled and Harry Stevenson recovered for ND. The half ended with the Trojans leading, 6–0.

There was no more scoring until the fourth quarter, when everyone broke loose. Notre Dame scored first when quarterback Bob Sheridan passed to John Kelly for a first down at the USC 10. It took Milt Piepul two carries to score, but he missed the extra point and made the score 6–6.

But USC came right back. With Lansdell carrying the ball seven out of eight times, from the Notre Dame 42-yard line, USC scored, Bob Jones added the extra point and the Trojans led, 13–6. The Irish took possession on their own 35-yard line after a penalty on the kickoff. Then, after a 5-yard penalty, halfback Ben Sheridan dashed 60 yards for the touchdown. John Kelleher missed the extra point, and the score was 13–12. USC got the ball back, and Ambrose Schindler romped 45 yards for a touchdown to ice the game, 20–12. USC was tied by UCLA the following week, but it finished 8-0-2, good enough to win Jones's fourth national championship.

In the locker room afterward, Jones said, "Notre Dame displayed the strongest attack we've met all year. I was glad when it was over." Jones had to savor the win because he never beat the Irish again. In fact, it would be eleven years before the Trojans would beat Notre Dame again.

## December 7, 1940:
## ND 10–USC 6 (L.A. Coliseum), 85,808

Cameron Applegate in *Notre Dame vs. USC* pointed out the similarities of ND coach Elmer Layden and USC coach Howard Jones: "Observing them on their respective benches as they coached their teams, you might have thought them carved out of the same chunk of granite. Both had volatile tempers which they controlled with difficulty but admirable success. Both were conservative, dedicated students and teachers of the game and on the 7th of December 1940, both coached their last football game."

Layden made his last year a good one, going out in style with a 7-2 record. Jones was not so fortunate. He finished 3-4-2, including the 10–6 loss to Notre Dame. Going into this game, the series stood 7-6-1 in Notre Dame's favor. And Jones, who would die of a heart attack in the summer following this season, had the fewest wins of his career at 3. USC had its moments of glory against Notre Dame since it would not win again for eleven years.

This game started off with the ND getting the ball after quarterback Bob Robertson's quick kick went out on the USC 48-yard line. Steve Juzwiak, Milt Piepul and Bob Saggau moved the ball to the Trojan 17, where Milt kicked a field goal for a 3–0 lead.

It didn't take long for the Trojans to respond. Robertson took the kickoff back 32 yards. Jack Banta carried for 11 to the Irish 47-yard line. Fullback Bobby Peoples eluded all Irish defenders and rumbled 46 yards for the score. Once more, sigh, the extra point was missed, and USC led, 6–3. Then the Notre Dame subs took over, much to Coach Jones's surprise. "I didn't think the Irish subs would drive 85 yards in 11 plays on us," he said. Led by Piepul, Notre Dame did exactly that, converting the extra point; then the scoring was done for the day.

A pass interference call gave USC first down on the Notre Dame 20 with only seconds to play, but the Trojans could not advance. The game ended with Layden incensed at the call. But when he asked Bernie Crimmins if he had shoved the USC guy, Bernie admitted that he had. Layden cooled down and went to apologize to the refs and to shake Howard Jones's hand more warmly for what he didn't know would be the last time.

# FRANK LEAHY (1-0) VS. SAM BARRY (0-1), 1941

## November 22, 1941:
## ND 20–USC 18 (L.A. Coliseum), 54,967

The story of Elmer Layden's departure has many facets. But the bottom line is that the administration, led by Vice-President John Cavanaugh, wanted to go in the proverbial new direction, so it turned to none other than Frank Leahy, another disciple of Rockne—so the direction was not *new* but at least new enough. Layden, meanwhile, "announced" that he was going to become commissioner of the National Football League at $20,000 per year. Everyone was happy—sort of—especially Frank Leahy. The new coach was an adamant devotee of Rockne, but he had enough sense and self-esteem to use Rockne's psychological ploys. He abandoned the famous "Notre Dame shift" in favor of the modern T formation. The result was unparalleled success and a winning percentage only second to Rockne among major college coaches, as well as more national championships than the Rock at four to three.

Meanwhile, USC turned to Sam Barry, already the head basketball and baseball coach. Barry took over all three duties simultaneously. It did not help that Jones had left the cupboard bare, and Barry finished 2-6-1. However, the only game the team was really out of was a 33–0 loss to Ohio State. Otherwise, USC seemed to improve and lost to a great Irish team only by 20–18.

USC scored first after blocking a Notre Dame punt and taking over on the Irish 33-yard line. USC stalled on the 20-yard line, but on fourth down, Bobby Robertson passed to Ralph Heywood for the TD. The extra point was blocked by Walt Ziemba, and the Trojans took a 6–0 lead.

In the second quarter, with USC trapped on its own 2-yard line, the Trojans punted and the Irish took over on the USC 33. After getting down to the 7-yard line, fullback Fred Evans crashed over for the score. Steve Juzwik kicked the extra point, and ND led, 7–6.

Then, on the next series of downs, Robertson fumbled, and Notre Dame recovered on its own 46. Behind the passing of Angelo Bertelli and the running of Juzwik, the Irish scored again but missed the conversion and led, 13–6. USC took over with six minutes left in the half, with the passing of Bob Musick leading the way. Then Musick lateraled to Bill Bledsoe, who scored. This time, John Kovatch blocked the extra point, and Notre Dame led at the half, 13–12.

Bertelli kept up his great passing in the third, completing three straight passes. Then, on the 17-yard line, he threw to Fred Evans in the flat, and Evans evaded three tacklers to score. Juzwik kicked the extra point, and the score was 20–12. But USC wasn't done. Late in the fourth quarter, Robertson went 8 yards off tackle to score. The game ended at 20–18 after a two-point conversion failed. Barry's short sojourn as coach ended as he went into the U.S. Navy for World War II, and Jeff Cravath took over as head

In 1941, Frank Leahy got his coaching career against USC off to a great start with a victory at home, 20–18, thanks to budding quarterback and future Heisman Trophy winner Angelo Bertelli. *ND Archives.*

coach. Leahy finished 8-0-1 and, strangely enough, did not win the national championship, which went to Minnesota, which went 8-0.

# FRANK LEAHY (4-1-1) VS. JEFF CRAVATH (1-4-1), 1942–1950

## November 28, 1942:
## ND 13–USC 0 (L.A. Coliseum), 94,519

Unfortunately, Jeff Cravath, who was a good coach, was outclassed by Leahy in the pair's six meetings (1-4-1). The last game before this monumental series was interrupted for three years by World War II was played before a huge crowd at the Coliseum. Leahy had a poor year by his standards, going

7-2-2, while new coach Cravath was 5-5-1, but of course, Leahy won again before leaving for two years to serve in the navy. The Irish went into the game 6-2-1, while USC had a mediocre 3-3-1.

Quarterback Angelo Bertelli saw that USC didn't win this day. He threw a touchdown pass to Creighton Miller for 48 yards in the first quarter, followed by a second one from the USC 12-yard line to Bob Livingston. After the extra point, it was 13–0, and the scoring was done for the day. USC made a final drive in the last period, but a Paul Taylor pass was intercepted by none other than Bertelli, ending the threat. Then the series was suspended for the next three years.

Leahy coached in 1943, losing only to the loaded Great Lakes Naval Station, and won his first national championship. Then he went into the navy for two years, while Ed McKeever took over in 1944 and Hughie Devore in 1945. Astonishingly, Leahy returned in 1946 and proceeded to go five years without losing a single game. Incredible. He finally lost to Purdue, 28–14, on October 7, 1950. Meanwhile, Cravath coached USC to forty-nine wins over eight years for an average of about six wins per year. Not bad, but it was no Leahy. In that same period, Frank lost five games, four of them in 1950.

Bob Dove, 1940–42, was voted a consensus all-American at Notre Dame in 1941. Of course, his teams never lost to the Trojans. *Collegiate Collection.*

NOTRE DAME VS. USC

Angelo Bertelli was a star from 1941 to 1943, winning the Heisman Trophy before he departed for military service. He never lost to USC. *Collegiate Collection.*

## November 30, 1946:
## ND 26–USC 6 (Notre Dame), 55,298

The two teams returned to the fray in 1946 at Notre Dame Stadium, with the Irish powerhouse winning, 26–6. Leahy won his second national championship as ND's record was marred only by a 0–0 tie with a dynamite Army team.

In this game, Coy McGee, a "little" 160-pound back, wreaked havoc. He took the opening kickoff eighty yards for a score, but the play was called back. That didn't stop him. Later in the second quarter, after a quick kick by USC, McGee ran 77 yards for a TD, and this one counted. The point after was missed, but it made little difference. After the Irish got the ball back, reserve quarterback George Ratterman led a 70-yard drive, culminating in his 22-yard pass to end Leon Hart for the score; Fred Early kicked the extra point, and Notre Dame led, 13–0, at half.

George Connor, often cited as the greatest player ever at Notre Dame, won the Outland Trophy as the nation's best interior lineman in 1946. He never lost to USC and is in the National Football Foundation Hall of Fame. *Collegiate Collection.*

The Trojans fought back in the third quarter. Led by quarterback George Murphy, they smashed their way to the 1-yard line. Halfback Johnny Naumu took it over for the score. The conversion was missed of course, and ND led, 13–6. But that was the end of the scoring for the men of Troy. The Irish tallied again when McGee (who else?) scored after a 60-yard drive. But when USC later punted, the Irish moved to the Trojan 25. Floyd Simmons gained 12, and then Gerry Cowhig took the pigskin over to make it 25–6. The final conversion sealed the easy victory and ND's No. 1 ranking.

## December 6, 1947:
## ND 38–USC 7 (L.A. Coliseum), 104,953

It only got worse for USC, as the Notre Dame juggernaut dominated college football, going undefeated and annihilating every team in its path,

All-American Johnny Lujack also won the Heisman Trophy and never lost to USC from 1943 to 1947. *Collegiate Collection.*

with its only relatively close game against Northwestern, 26–19. Many consider the 1947 team—which featured Heisman-winning quarterback Johnny Lujack, tackle George Connor, halfback Emil Sitko, halfback Terry Brennan, tackle Ziggy Czarobski, future Heisman winner Leon Hart, backup quarterback and future pro great Frank Tripucka, left end Jim Martin and left guard Bill Fischer—to be the greatest team ever. The Irish massacred the Trojans, 38–7. The Irish scoring included two touchdowns from Sitko—1 yard and 76 yards—a 98-yard run by Bob Livingstone and a 72-yard rumble by tackle Alfred Zmijewski after he intercepted a lateral. It was the worst defeat for USC since the series started and helped give Leahy his third national championship.

## December 4, 1948:
## ND 14–USC 14 (L.A. Coliseum), 100,571

Well, well. It looks like it is time for revenge. Another great Irish team ambled into the Coliseum (the game was played in the Coliseum for the second straight year to get the series back on its regular schedule—odd years in South Bend and even in Los Angeles) after having just defeated Washington the previous week by 46–0, and it was promptly hogtied, 14–14, by a decidedly inferior 6-3 Trojan team, giving the national championship to ND's archcompetitor, Michigan. Leahy had not lost a game since he was beaten by the same Michigan team on November 14, 1942, 32–20. But USC was up to the task.

"The three-touchdown underdogs outcharged, outfought and nearly outscored the South Bend Supermen," Applegate reported. The Irish ended up losing six of seven fumbles, and USC punting kept them at bay. However, all-American Leon Hart caught a pass from Frank Tripucka and was hit four times on the way to the goal, but he escaped each time and scored. Applegate noted that "trying to tackle Hart was like trying to bulldog a full grown Brahma bull." The conversion made the score 7–0. Things then went back and forth, with USC holding its own. In the fourth quarter, Dill faded to pass but, seeing the receivers covered, raced to

Bill Fischer, 1945–48, was a two-time consensus all-American guard, rated as the best in Notre Dame history. His teams never lost to USC. *Collegiate Collection.*

the 6-yard line. Art Battle and Bill Martin helped get the ball down to the one before Martin scored standing up. Dill's kick was good, and the score was 7–7. With the end of the game coming, Kirby took a Williams punt and carried it to the Notre Dame 42. Dill passed to Ernie Tolman for a first down on the 18. Martin and Battle again led the charge down to the four, where Martin scored. The conversion put USC ahead, 14–7.

But the Irish were not done. Gay took the kickoff and ran all the way to the USC 13-yard line. Pass interference was called on Gene Beck, and the Irish were on the 2-yard line. Emil Sitko slashed over the right guard, and Steve Oracko tied the score with a perfect kick. The Trojans came close, but the Irish, riding a twenty-eight-game winning streak, were confident even when they were behind with little time.

Applegate reported in his book:

> As USC lined up to kick to Notre Dame after their touchdown drive, Billy Gay calmly walked over to the referee and asked: "Mr. Referee, how much time is left?"
>
> "Two minutes and 35 seconds," the referee replied.
>
> "Thank you sir, that's enough," Gay said, and ran that kickoff back 86 yards to set up the final TD.

## November 26, 1949:
## ND 32–USC 0 (Notre Dame), 57,214

Notre Dame had to regroup in 1949. After all, it had lost 1 and tied 2 games for Leahy since 1942. Frank had enough of that, and they promptly went undefeated and won his fourth national championship in the decade dominated by Notre Dame. USC, meanwhile, was 5-2-1 going into the game against the Irish—chopped liver. Notre Dame annihilated the Trojans, 32–0, before a full house. ND's only remotely close game of the season came the following week, when it beat SMU, 27–20.

The first touchdown was a 40-yard pass from Williams to Hart. Then halfback John Pettibon caught a ball tipped to him by USC halfback Pat Duff, and he raced 40 yards for the second score. Then Sitko blasted 5 yards off tackle for the third TD before the half ended. Substitute half Frank Spaniel scored on a 13-yard run in the second half. The fifth and final touchdown was scored by halfback Bill Barrett crashing over center after just having caught a 31-yard pass. It was a sad day for the Trojans in more ways

Jim Martin was a four-year starter at Notre Dame from 1946 to 1949 at tackle. ND won three national championships in that period, and of course, he never lost to USC. *Collegiate Collection.*

than one. The day before the game, Colonel Orv Mohler, the all-American quarterback from 1930, was killed when the B-25 he was piloting developed engine trouble and crashed in Alabama. He was forty years old.

## December 2, 1950:
## USC 9–ND 7 (L.A. Coliseum), 70,177

Holy cow! Coach Frank Leahy was human after all. He had the worst record of his career in 1950, going 4-4-1, and also losing to USC the only time in his career. It was also Jeff Cravath's only win against the Irish as he bowed out as coach with his worst season, at 2-5-2. But he had to face Notre Dame after suffering a humiliating 39–0 beating from archenemy UCLA the previous week. But USC, according to Applegate, "attacked the Irish like a pride of famished lions." Nine Notre Dame players were injured, and USC triumphed, 9–7.

The Irish scored first in the second quarter, as quarterback Williams took his squad 54 yards and scored himself from a yard out. The extra point was good, and the Irish led, 7–0. But that was it for the day. Thirty seconds later, Jim Sears raced 94 yards for a TD. Frank Gifford—yeah, *the* Frank Gifford—converted, and the score was tied, 7–7. It was a fierce battle in the second half. Finally, Paul McMurtry, a thirty-one-year-old guard from Texas, tore through the line and blocked a ND kick. Tackle Volney Peters recovered it in the end zone for a two-point safety and a Trojan victory. "Leahy also treated the Trojans as though they were some scrub team from the hinterlands. He won eight, lost one and tied one. And three days after his 1950 loss to the Trojans, USC fired coach Jeff Cravath," wrote Bisheff and Schrader.

# FRANK LEAHY (3-0) VS. JESS HILL (0-3), 1951–1953

## December 1, 1951:
## ND 19–USC 12 (L.A. Coliseum), 55,783

All-around athlete Jesse T. Hill—former major-league baseball player, freshman football coach and track coach—was a surprise choice to succeed Cravath but not a bad one. Even though he finished 2-4 against the Irish (0-3 against Leahy), his record for six years was a solid 45-17-1. He started the 1951 season with seven straight victories before losing the last three games. Meanwhile, the Irish, who recovered a little after the 1950 season, were 6-2-1 when they faced USC.

The first half was scoreless, but the Trojans came out after intermission behind halfback Frank Gifford, who scored from 8 yards out, but Frank missed the extra point, and the Trojans led, 6–0. Notre Dame retaliated quickly behind eighteen-year-old freshman quarterback sensation Ralph Guglielmi. He threw passes for 13, 10 and 35 yards for a first down on the USC 15. Future Heisman Trophy winner Johnny Lattner carried the ball in for the first Irish TD. Bob Joseph blew the extra point, and the score was even at half.

The Trojans came out after intermission, and Dick Nunis promptly intercepted a Guglielmi pass and carried it to the Irish 34. Dean Schneider passed to halfback Jim Sears for first down on the five. Sears scored on the next play, and the Trojans led, 12–6, after Frank again—keeping with a Trojan tradition—missed the extra point. Near the end of the period, the Irish mounted a strong ground attack behind Lattner and fullback Neil Worden. They marched 73 yards and tied the score, 12–12. Joseph, too, missed the extra point.

USC came back with a great drive to the Irish 8, but a touchdown pass to five-foot-six Cosaimo Cutri failed, and the Irish took over behind Guglielmi, Lattner, Worden and Pettibon, scoring again and converting. The final score was 19–12 in ND's favor. The most remarkable thing about the game was that all-American halfback Johnny Lattner said that he got to visit Marilyn Monroe in her dressing room Friday before the game, according to Bisheff and Schrader.

Leahy made his usual postgame locker room speech "sound like a prince of the Holy Roman Empire thanking his crusaders for vanquishing an army of Saracens." Writer Joe Doyle said that when he covered Notre Dame, he never knew whether to say hello to Leahy or genuflect.

## November 30, 1952:
## ND 9–USC 0 (Notre Dame), 58,394

The year 1952 promised to be a big one for USC. It went into South Bend 9-0 and ranked No. 1 in the country. But Notre Dame wasn't chopped liver either. It had a 6-2-1 record, unremarkable for a Leahy team but with wins over excellent teams from Oklahoma, Texas and Purdue. It wasn't long before USC was added to that list.

The only touchdown was scored by Johnny Lattner on a buck into the line in the first quarter. After missing the conversion, ND kicked a field goal from the 17-yard line in the third quarter, and the game finished 9–0. The Trojans' season was somewhat salvaged with a victory over UCLA the previous week and a victory over Wisconsin in the Rose Bowl, 7–0. But Notre Dame finished third in the final polls and USC fifth.

## November 28, 1953:
## ND 48–USC 14 (L.A. Coliseum), 97,952

Jesse Hill's last shot against Notre Dame also did not bear any fruits of victory. Notre Dame, with a 7-0-1 record, beat USC, 48–14, a farewell gift to Leahy, also in his last year. An undefeated season and a No. 2 ranking in the final polls (second only to undefeated Maryland) did not prohibit Notre Dame's administration from ousting Leahy. Nobody's job is safe in football—college or pro.

USC, meanwhile, was 6-2-1 going into this game, having just lost to the Gutty Little Bruins, 13–0. But Notre Dame was a powerhouse. "One writer," Applegate reported, "was of the opinion that if the entire first team was named All-American there would have been little argument. The consensus was that the 1953 backfield of Guglielmi, Worden, Heap and Lattner was every bit the equal and in some ways superior to the Four Horsemen of 1930."

In the first quarter, halfback Joe Heap took a punt on his 7-yard line and romped 93 yards for the score and a 6–0 lead when Guglielmi missed the conversion. On Notre Dame's next series, it went 61 yards, culminating with Johnny Lattner going 9 yards around left end for the score. The conversion made it 13–0. But USC came back when left half Des Koch returned a punt 43 yards to the Irish 31. From there, the Trojans marched to the goal line, with Koch scoring from 3 yards out. Sam Tsaglakis kicked the extra point, making it 13–7, but not for long. Four plays after the ensuing kickoff, topped by Neil Worden's 55-yard run up the middle, Notre Dame took a 20–7 lead following Worden's 2-yard run.

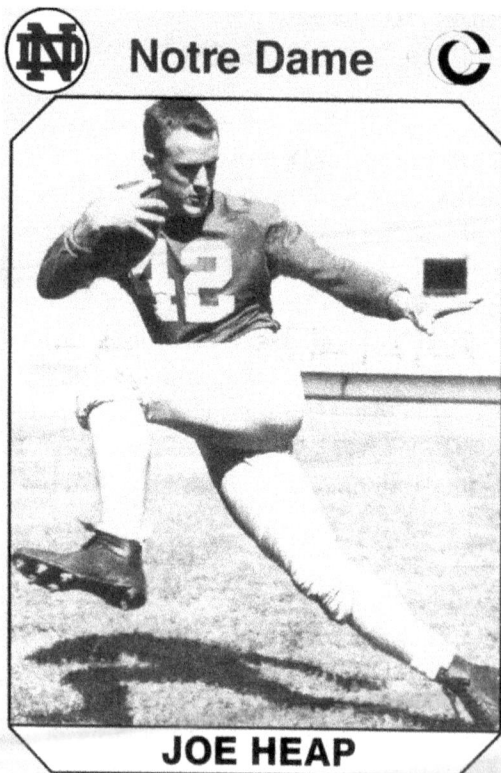

**Notre Dame** C

**JOE HEAP**

Joe Heap was part of what was regarded as the best backfield of all time in 1953—Johnny Lattner, Ralph Gugliemi and Neil Worden were the others. Heap teams beat USC four straight years. *Collegiate Collection.*

The Games

In the third quarter, Lattner and Guglielmi pushed the Irish to a 27–7 lead, but USC came back with halfback Aramis Dandoy scoring from 12 yards out. But Notre Dame answered with Lattner (who else?) scoring his third touchdown of the day from the one. ND's sixth TD of the day came on a Dandoy miscue behind his own goal, with the Irish recovering for six points. Lattner closed out the scoring and the game with his fourth touchdown, 48–14. The series stood at 16-7-2 Notre Dame.

# TERRY BRENNAN (1-2) VS. JESS HILL (2-1), 1954–1956

## November 27, 1954:
## ND 23–USC 17 (Notre Dame), 56,438

Terry Brennan at twenty-five years old became one of the youngest football coaches in America to inherit a major football program. A former halfback for Leahy, it was now his turn to take on Hill, but Jesse triumphed 2-1. In the first game, USC came in 8-2 and the Irish 7-1, but Notre Dame prevailed, 23–17. It probably didn't help that the Trojans had lost the previous week to UCLA by a score of 34–0. Notre Dame did not help itself by fumbling three times, all recovered by center Marv Goux. After taking over on the Irish 14-yard line, Aramis Dandoy scored from the 3, and the score was 6–1. Sam Tsagalakis converted.

In the second quarter, the Irish were backed up on their own 4-yard line. A Joe Heap punt allowed the Trojans to take over on the 20. But the Irish got tough, and Tsagalakis missed a field goal. The Irish took over and proceeded to march 80 yards for the tying touchdown. The biggest gainer was Joe Heap, running through the line for 39 yards. The Irish tallied when Heap passed to Jim Morse, who went over standing up, 7–7.

In the second half, Dandoy led a charge down to the Irish 13, but Notre Dame held, so Tsagalakis kicked a 24-yard field goal. Eventually, the Trojans had to punt, and the Irish marched 106 yards (86 yards plus 20 yards in penalties) in thirteen plays and ten minutes. Now the Irish led, 14–10, but not for long. USC quarterback Jim Contratto came in and completed five straight passes, including the final to end Chuck Griffith for the touchdown.

A consensus all-American in 1954, Ralph Guglielmi led the team in passing for three consecutive years and beat USC three consecutive times. *Collegiate Collection.*

Now the Trojans led, 17–14, with ten and a half minutes remaining. But Guglielmi threw a short pass to Jim Morse, who raced 72 yards for the winning touchdown. A safety made the final score 23–17. The Irish ended up with four all-Americans—Joe Heap, Ralph Guglielmi, Dan Shannon and Frank Verrichione—as well as No. 4 ranking in the final poll. But USC did not do badly, finishing at No. 17.

## November 26, 1955:
## USC 42–ND 20 (L.A. Coliseum), 94,892

Notre Dame was 8-1 going into the USC game, and the Trojans were 5-4. No contest, right? Well, it *was* no contest…on USC's part, as it ran away with a 42–20 victory. The Irish were ranked fifth, but USC came out and scored 21 points in eighteen minutes. Junior quarterback Ellsworth Kissinger took USC 68 yards in eleven plays. Ellwsworth took the ball over from the 1 and made the conversion. But the Irish came right back, going 67 yards in eleven plays behind all-American quarterback Paul Hornung. The Golden Boy himself carried the ball the last 8 yards, bulling into the end zone. Paul kicked the extra point, and the score was tied, 7–7.

Now USC, behind its own all-American back, Jon Arnett, moved the ball to the 15-yard line at the end of the quarter. Kissinger passed to fullback C.R. Roberts for the score, and the Trojans led, 14–7, after Arnett converted. After the kickoff, Notre Dame's Dick Fitzgerald fumbled, and USC's George Galli recovered on the ND 21. Six plays later, Arnett scored the third touchdown, with Bob Isackson converting for a 21–7 lead. Notre Dame, however, came right back, with Hornung throwing a pass to Jim Morse for 78 yards and a TD. Hornung missed the conversion, and USC led, 21–13.

Hornung drove the Irish again to the 3-yard line, but the Irish fumbled, and USC recovered in the end zone for a touchback. Then Hornung passed to Morse for 60 yards, Notre Dame scored, and the tally was 21–20 after Paul kicked the extra point. But that was all the scoring for the Irish. Contratto completed a pass to Arnett on the Irish 26, and Arnett took it into the end zone. He kicked the extra point and made it 28–20. Following a critical interception by USC, the Trojans scored again for a 35–20 lead. Then another Hornung pass was intercepted by Ben Sampson on the USC 21. Four plays later, the Trojans were leading 42–20, the final score. Notre Dame dropped to eighth in the final poll, and USC was happy to end the season with a win.

## December 1, 1956:
## USC 28–ND 20 (L.A. Coliseum), 64,538

This was a year of controversy. Frank Leahy got all over Terry Brennan for coaching blunders. The Irish were 2-7, their worst all-time record, going into the USC game. USC, meanwhile, had been penalized by the National Collegiate Athletic Association (NCAA) because the Southern California Education Foundation gave players forty-five dollars per game. Jon Arnett was among them, and he was only allowed to play in five games.

Regardless, because of ND's poor record, Socal was a two-touchdown favorite. The Trojans marched from their own 34, and Jim Conroy took it around right end to score. Kissinger converted, and USC led, 7–0. But the Irish came right back, going 76 yards in ten plays, with Bob Williams scoring from the six. But Hornung missed the extra point. USC drove from its own

23-yard line down to the Irish 15. Then fullback C.R. Roberts hit end Hillard Hill in the end zone for a TD. Tailback Rex Johnston converted for a 14–6 lead. But the Irish came back, with Williams throwing a 10-yard strike to Bob Ward in the end zone, making it 14–13. USC returned the favor, marching down the field and allowing Conroy to throw touchdown pass to Don Voyne from the 15-yard line, making it 21–13. But Hornung caught a punt and raced 95 yards for the return score, making it 21 20 USC, with two minutes to play. The Trojans were not done. Taking the ball on his own 38, Ernie Zampese rolled 62 yards for a score, and the final tally was 28–20.

# Terry Brennan (2-0) vs. Don Clark (0-2), 1957–1958

## November 30, 1957:
## ND 40–USC 12 (Notre Dame), 54,793

Terry Brennan, the young Irish coach, went into his third season with high hopes. Sure, he had finished 2-8 the previous year, but he had gone 9-1 and 8-2 his first two years. He went into the USC game with a 5-3 record. The bright side was that two weeks earlier, the Irish had ended Oklahoma's 47-game winning streak, 7–0, in Oklahoma no less. No matter—this was a new game. Meanwhile, USC was having a horrible time. Don Clark was 1-8 and going nowhere fast.

This game was no better. The Irish started out strong when Bob Williams intercepted a pass and carried it to the USC 27. Six plays later, fullback Ron Toth scored from the six. Monty Stickles missed the extra point, and ND led, 6–0. Then USC fumbled on its own 32. Charles Puntillo recovered, and Williams threw to Frank Reynolds on the 17 and then to Stickles for the touchdown, making it 13–0. Things turned for USC when the Irish fumbled on their own 22, and USC recovered. The Trojans moved to the 10, and Rex Johnson went over right end for the score. But USC kicked off, and Pat Doyle returned it 92 yards for a touchdown. It was 19–6 at the half.

Then, in the third quarter, halfback Jim Crotty carried the ball five times in an Irish 66-yard-drive, ending with him scoring. Stickles made the kick, making it 26–6. But USC came back, sort of. Quarterback Tom Maudlin scored from the six-inch line after 67-yard drive. In the last quarter, Williams threw a 7-yard pass to Stickles for the TD, and then reserve George Ito finished an 80-yard drive with a TD pass to Dick Pendergast. The final was 40–12.

## November 29, 1958:
## ND 20–USC 13 (L.A. Coliseum), 66,903

The year 1958 was not a banner one for Terry Brennan. He went 6-4 and was fired. Notre Dame went into its annual match with a 5-4 record, while USC was even worse at 4-4-1. The Irish jumped off to a 6–0 lead when fullback Nick Pietrosante went over from the 1-yard line. But the Trojans answered immediately with a 41-yard TD pass by Don Buford to Hilliard Hill and a 7–6 lead. In the second quarter, halfback Jerry Traynham scored from 1 yard out to end a 34-yard Trojan drive. Don Zachik converted for a 13–6 lead, but it didn't last long. Williams capped a 70s-yard drive with a TD run, but Stickles missed the conversion, so it was 13–12. But veteran Williams went in for Izo and led the Irish to an 18–13 lead with a pass to Bob Wetoska. Williams made a two-point conversion on a throw to Crotty, and it was 20–13 ND. USC made some noble attempts, but the game ended at that score.

# Joe Kuharich (1-0) vs. Don Clark (0-1), 1959

## November 28, 1959:
## ND 16–USC 6 (Notre Dame), 48,682

Terry Brennan spent five years as Irish coach and finished 32-18. He was fired at the beginning of 1957, apparently because of pressure from the alumni. It was strange because the administration was trying to deemphasize football, so why deemphasize Terry Brennan?

The national media didn't agree much with the decision. Arthur Daly of the *New York Times* said that Notre Dame made an "outrageous botch of the job." Syndicate columnist Red Smith wrote that "nobody questioned Brennan's fitness as a leader of young men. In short, there seems to have been no conceivable reason for his dismissal except that his team did not win all the time." Even Father Theodore Hesburgh sided with Brennan, but he apparently was not strong enough to resist the alumni.

So Joe Kuharich, a National Football League (NFL) coach and former guard under Elmer Layden, was hired. It turned out to be the worst decision in Notre Dame history. Kuharich went 17-23 in four years and never seemed to impress anyone—players, fans or fellow coaches. But he was successful, for some reason, against the Trojans. He went 3-1 and won his first game in 1959, 16–6. Kuharich went into the game with a shoddy 4-5 record.

Don Clark in his last year at USC had his best season, going into the game 8-1. "Yet the attack of the alumni was relentless and merciless," Applegate reported in *Notre Dame Vs. USC.* It was so bad that Clark just decided to quit and go into business. (He died in 1989 at age sixty-five after suffering a heart attack jogging.)

Meanwhile, the 1959 game had to be played. After some exchanges, ND took over on the Trojan 38. Fullback Gerry Gray carried the ball to the 13-yard line, where he fumbled, and Nick Buoniconti recovered for the Irish. Gray then went over for the first touchdown, and Monty Stickles converted for a 7–0 lead. Nothing much happened until the third quarter, when Irish quarterback George Izo drove the Irish 49 yards, with Gray eventually smashing over tackle for the second score. Monty converted again, and it was 14–0. Halfback Angelo Coia was trapped in the end zone on the following kickoff, and the Irish added a safety to their total, making it 16–0. USC finally scored when Ben Charles came in and led the Trojans on an 84-yard march that culminated in a touchdown pass to Coia. The final score was 16–6.

# JOE KUHARICH (2-1) VS. JOHN MCKAY (1-2), 1960–1962

## November 26, 1960:
## ND 17–USC 0 (L.A. Coliseum), 28,297

Life is a strange business. Joe Kuharich, a mediocre coach at best, faced John McKay USC teams three times—the first two he won by a combined total of 47–0. There has to be reasons for it. The main one seems to be that USC was having down years, and McKay was getting acclimated to his new job. Kuharich was 2-8 in 1960 (the worst ND record ever) and had lost eight games in a row when he took his team to Los Angeles to play the Trojans and won 17–0. Imagine how McKay felt. They were 4-5 when they faced the Irish. Nobody was too excited about the game. It rained. About 45,000 tickets were sold, but only 28,297 showed up. The USC fans, at least, should have stayed home.

Notre Dame was in charge from the beginning. Angelo Dabiero took the opening kickoff to the 29, and quarterback Daryl Lamonica moved the Irish steadily downfield, where they stalled on the USC 21, so Joe Perkowski kicked a field goal. After ND kicked off, Bill Nelson's pass was intercepted by Lamonica (notice that guys were still playing two ways in 1960), who returned it to the USC 45. Then Daryl completed one of the two passes he threw all day long for 18 yards to the 1-yard line. There he plunged over for the score, and it was 10–0, with the game not eleven minutes old. Halfway through the second period, the Irish drove 80 yards to the USC 9. Halfback Scarpitto scored to make it 17–0 after the Perkowski extra point. That was that. Both sides finished out the second half cold and wet and were glad that the game was over. So were the fans. That was John McKay's welcome to the Notre Dame–USC warfare.

## October 14, 1961:
## ND 30–USC 0 (Notre Dame), 50,427

The next year did not fare any better. Injuries had decimated USC, and ten players were either sidelined or severely hampered. Notre Dame was looking better. After opening wins over Oklahoma and Purdue, the faithful were starting to have visions of Leahy and Rockne (big mistake). The 30–0 drubbing of the Trojans did not diminish their ardor (though the rest of the season did).

Lamonica scored on a 12-yard run after a 55-yard drive. Lamonica threw a 19-yard TD pass to Jim Kelly. Fullback Perkowski scored after an 84-yard drive, and it was 20–0 before USC could catch its breath. It never did. In the second half, Lamonica again went over from the 1-yard line. Later Perkowski kicked a 49-yard field goal to close out the scoring and the game.

"We're a better team than we looked," deadpanned McKay. Really? He finished 4-5-1.

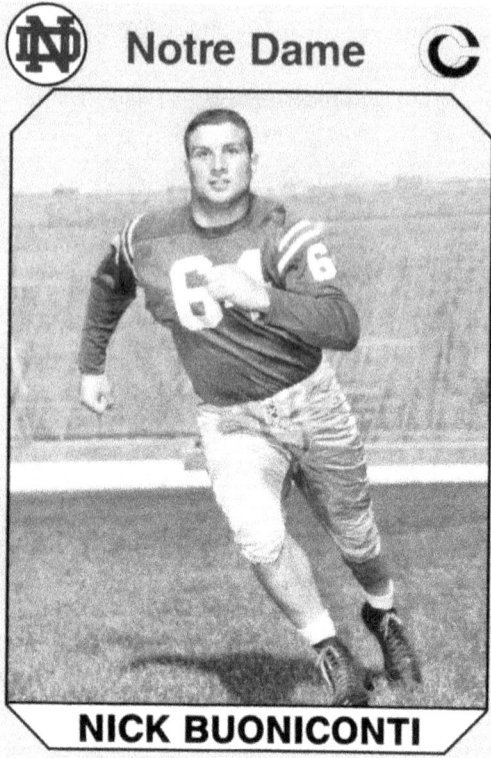

**NICK BUONICONTI**

Linebacker Nick Buoniconti was first-team all-American in 1961. A highlight of his senior season was a 30–0 victory over USC. *Collegiate Collection.*

## December 1, 1962:
## USC 25–ND 0 (L.A. Coliseum), 81,676

Finally, to McKay's delight, it suddenly was a Trojan horse of a different color. Talk about turning things around. The Trojans went undefeated (11-0) in 1962, their best year under McKay, not counting his 12-0 year in 1972. How did they do it? The answer was simple: players. Quarterback Pete Beathard, end Hal Bedsole, guard Damon Bame, tackle Marv Marinovich, fullback Ben Wilson, guard Pete Lubisch and halfbacks Wilie Brown, Ken Del Conte and Jay Clark all had their way with the Irish. Notre Dame had lost four straight to Big Ten opponents before it won four straight coming into Los Angeles. Beathard and Brown drove Trojans down to the 18 and made more yardage before Wilson scored from the one. Tom Lupo kicked the extra point, and USC led, 7–0. Then the Trojans recovered an Irish fumble on their own 22 and carried it all the way. Next, Wilson scored from the ND 14, and USC led, 13–0, at half after the two-point conversion failed.

After the half, Notre Dame had to punt, and Del Conte ran the ball back to the Irish 40. The backs hammered their way to the 14 before Bill Nelson threw a touchdown pass to Fred Hill. In the last quarter, Nelson completed a pass to Fred Hill, who scored. After an interception, Craig Fertig, third-string quarterback, led USC on a drive, scoring himself on a 6-yard run, making the final score 25–0 and ensuring the national championship for USC.

"Some people—a lot of people—doubted we were No. 1," said USC fullback Ben Wilson. "If you know anybody who still does, tell him I'd appreciate meeting him outside after we're through here," reported Rappoport in his book. Meanwhile, Kuharich had had enough, being expected to win every game. On March 13, 1963, just before spring practice, he said that he was quitting. The alumni at least, were relieved, and Kuharich went back to the pros.

# Hugh Devore (1-0) vs. John McKay (1-0), 1963

## October 12, 1963:
## ND 17–USC 14 (Notre Dame), 59,135

John McKay had a one-year respite before having to face Ara Parseghian, his counterpart as the two best college coaches of their era. Unfortunately for John, Hughie Devore took over for one year as an interim coach and still beat USC, but he wanted to have the best year possible. Unfortunately, that meant only two wins—one over UCLA and the other over USC. Talk about embarrassing. The Californians had to be red-faced since they finished 7-3.

This game started with an Irish fumble early in the first quarter. Mike Garrett recovered on the Notre Dame 45. Beathard bounced a pass off Bedsole's fingertips into the waiting hands of Irish halfback Tommy MacDonald (not *the* Tommy McDonald of Oklahoma), who took it all the way to the house. Ken Ivan converted, and ND led, 7–0. But the

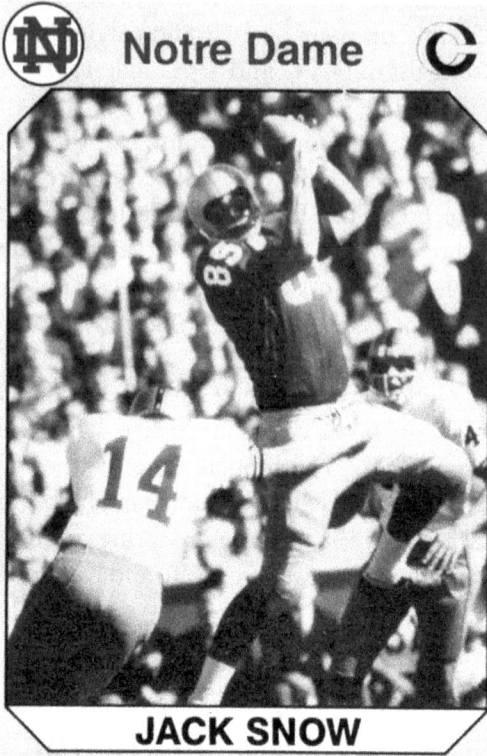

**Notre Dame**

**JACK SNOW**

End Jack Snow was a great player for the Irish from 1962 to 1964 and for the Los Angeles Rams in the NFL. He lost two out of three decisions to USC, but he always made an impact on the games. *Collegiate Collection.*

Trojans, spearheaded by Beathard and Garrett, marched 74 yards to a score, and Dick Brownell made the point after, 7–7. In the second period, halfback Bill Wolski returned the kickoff 30 yards. He then went 36 yards over the middle to the USC 8. Wolski also carried the final 6 yards, Ivan kicked the extra point and ND led, 14–7. But USC came back and went 93 yards, Brownell converted and the score was 14–14 at the half.

The second half was all defense. With six minutes and twenty-eight seconds to play, Ivan, now known as Ivan the Terrible to USC, kicked a 33-yard field goal to put ND ahead. That was enough. The final score was 17–14 ND. That was also it for Hughie Devore, one of the most popular coaches ever. He moved to assistant athletic director, making room for you know who.

# Ara Parseghian (3-6-2) vs. John McKay (6-3-2), 1964–1974

## November 28, 1964:
## USC 20–ND 17 (L.A. Coliseum), 83,840

Only a true Notre Dame fan could appreciate the arrival of Ara Parseghian as leader of the pack. In spite of Rockne, Leahy, Devine and Holtz, this handsome, charismatic, talented coach still remains the favorite of many Irish fans. Even the fact that he was not Catholic was not held against him. It did not hurt that he finished his eleven years with a record of 95-17-4—not exactly bad. The sour news for his fans was that he was only 3-6-2 against McKay. Why? That's a good question. Both men were among the best coaches of their day. Both men had superior talent to work with. Both men had the support of their administration and fans. Why did John prevail? Who knows? That's the way the football tumbles.

One of the biggest wins of all time for USC came in 1964, when it rallied from a 17–0 rout to win the game 20–17 and spoil Notre Dame's chances for a national championship in Parseghian's first year. Incredibly, Ara's team had beaten Wisconsin, Purdue, Air Force, UCLA, Stanford, Navy, Pittsburgh, Michigan State and Iowa with almost the same players who had finished 2-7 the year before. Meanwhile, USC had lost to Michigan State, Ohio State and Washington. It didn't matter. This one turned into a barnburner.

It all started innocently enough, with Notre Dame dominating the first half. After Rod Sherman fumbled from a hard hit by halfback Tom Longo, and ND's Don Gmitter recovered, quarterback John Huarte went to work. He threw to Phil Sheridan for 16 yards and to Nick Eddy for 22. After the Trojans held them, Ken Ivan kicked a 25-yard field goal. Passing to Jack Snow and Sheridan, the Irish marched downfield, where Huarte delivered to Snow in the end zone for six. Ivan converted for a 10–0 lead. The Trojans made a gallant attempt but stalled on the 16-yard line of Notre Dame and had to give the ball up on downs.

But Jim Walker intercepted a Huarte pass, and USC tried again but failed. Notre Dame took over, and this time Huarte marched the men down the field in eleven plays, with Bill Wolski running the ball in from 5 yards out. Ivan converted once more, and it was 17–0 at half—lights out for USC.

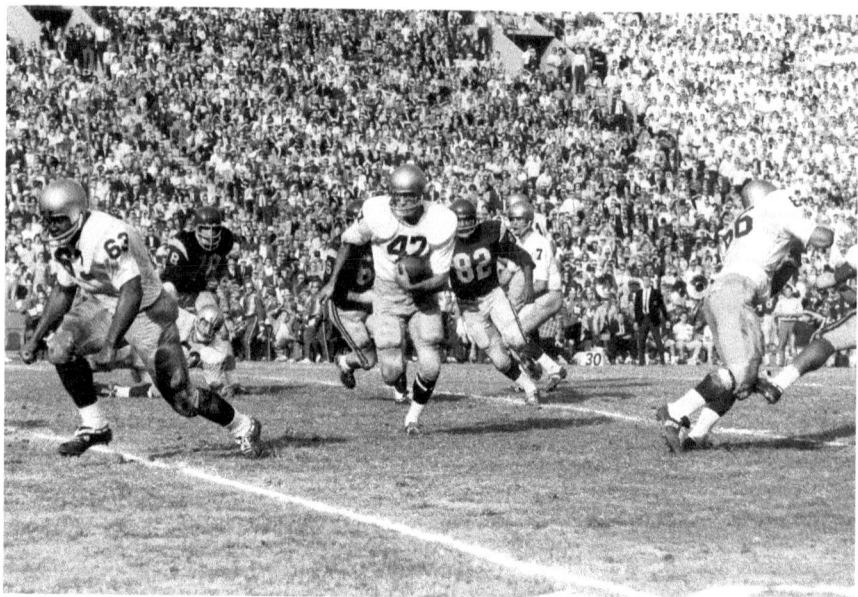

Another one of USC's greatest victories came in 1964 and prevented its undefeated (up to then) archrival from winning the national championship. Down 17–0, the Trojans rallied and went ahead on a pass from Craig Fertig to Rod Sherman. The final score was 20–17. *ND Archives.*

"Our game plan is working," McKay told his troops at halftime, as noted by Rappoport. "Keep doing your stuff, and we'll get some points. I knew we had them. The momentum was all ours. In a situation like that, a No. 1 rating is a fairly suffocating thing." Notre Dame didn't score again.

After the kickoff, quarterback Craig Fertig drove the Trojans 66 yards in ten plays. Mike Garrett eventually went over from the one, Dick Brownell converted and it was 17–7. Then the Trojans stalled, and Huarte took over on the ND 34 and rolled down the field. Fullback Joe Cantor scored from the one, but a holding penalty called it back. The Irish decided to go for it on fourth down and failed, and USC took over on its own 12. Fertig took over again, moving the Trojans 88 yards downfield for the score. The TD pass for 23 yards went to end Fred Hill, but Brownell missed the conversion, 17–13.

When the Irish could not get anywhere, USC took over on the ND forty with two minutes and ten seconds to play. Fertig marched the Trojans downfield again. A touchdown pass to Hill in the end zone was ruled out of bounds. On the next play, Irish all-American end Alan Page crushed Fertig, who fumbled— so the Irish faithful claimed—but the ref called it an incomplete pass. Fertig got another chance and passed to Sherman for the touchdown, and Brownell kicked the extra point, 20–17. With one minute and thirty-three seconds left, Notre Dame could go nowhere, and all was lost: the game, the undefeated season and the national championship. It was one of USC's favorite victories of all time, especially considering it was the Irish.

"The thing that struck me was the great presence of Parseghiam," said Tom Pagna, longtime ND radio announcer of the Irish games and one of Ara's top assistants. "The kids were absolutely devastated. Ara told them if they wanted to kick a locker, punch a towel or say a profanity, to go ahead and get it out of their systems. 'Then we're going to let the press in and act like gentlemen, with no excuses,' he said," according to *Fight On!* As for USC, the Trojans were upset, too, when Oregon State was invited to the Rose Bowl instead of them.

## October 23, 1965:
## ND 28–USC 7 (Notre Dame), 59,235

Well, it didn't take long for Ara to exact revenge. The bouts in 1965 and 1966 were two of the worst losses that USC ever suffered against

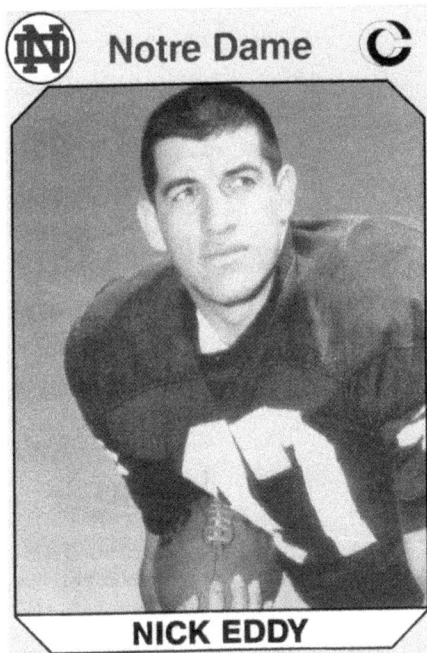

**Notre Dame**

**NICK EDDY**

Notre Dame. In 1965, the Trojans had won four straight, while Notre Dame had a 3-1 record, having lost to Purdue. The Irish defense reigned, shutting down Mike Garrett almost completely. Meanwhile, Larry Conjar, ND's sophomore fullback, scored four touchdowns and ran for 116 yards, 73 more than Garrett. Conjar and Bill Wolski went up the middle

Nick Eddy was a first-team all-American halfback in 1966, and he was on Irish teams that beat USC two out of three. *Collegiate Collection.*

Alan Page was one of the greatest players ever for Notre Dame. He was a consensus all-American defensive end in 1966 and was on teams that won two out of three from the Trojans. *Collegiate Collection.*

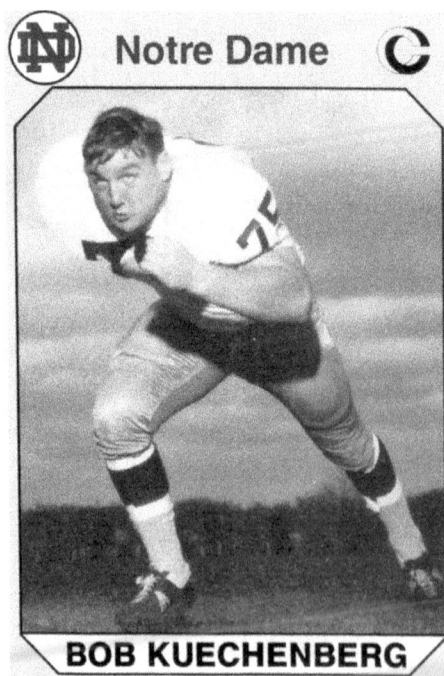

Defensive tackle Bob Kuechenberg was a star for Notre Dame and the NFL Miami Dolphins for fourteen years. He was on the team that demolished USC, 51–0, in 1966. *Sporting News Archives.*

for 45 yards in ten plays for the first touchdown. Then, after a penalty, they went 40 yards in eight plays, and Conjar scored again. In the second quarter, Conjar led a 67-yard charge that ended in a third touchdown and a 21–0 halftime lead. In the third quarter, the Irish went another 67 yards, with Conjar scoring for a 28–0 lead. Finally, USC came back for its only touchdown as John Thomas caught a pass from Troy Winslow for the final score and a 28–7 ND win. McKay and Parseghian ended the season with identical 7-2-1 records. The Irish finished ranked ninth and USC tenth.

## November 26, 1966:
## ND 51–USC 0 (L.A. Coliseum), 88,520

November 26, 1966, had to be the most embarrassing football day that McKay ever spent. Notre Dame, operating with a second-string quarterback, Coley O'Brien, massacred USC and the Trojan horse, 51–0, in their home corral—the worst defeat in the long rivalry. This was the first USC-ND game

Reserve quarterback Coley O'Brien led Notre Dame to stunning 51–0 victory over the Trojans in 1966 at the Coliseum. It helped earn Ara his first national championship. *ND Archives.*

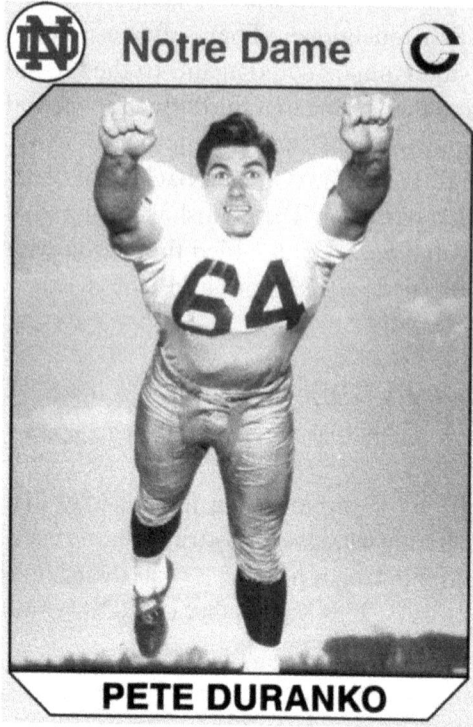

Defensive tackle Pete Duranko was an all-American in 1966 as part of a defense that recorded six shutouts in ten games. His teams beat the Trojans three out of four times. *Collegiate Collection.*

I ever attended. Paul Zimmerman, sports editor of the *Los Angeles Times*, wrote before the game, "It could be a low scoring contest, bringing together two of the top ranked defensive units of the land." Right…well, at least *one* top-ranked defensive unit. Notre Dame made short work of USC, scoring on drives of 80, 72, 64, 41, 39 and 38 yards, and two pass interceptions contributed to the devastation. Joe Azzaro kicked a 38-yard field goal and six extra points.

After the game, McKay told his players in the locker room, "Forget it guys; do you realize there are 700 million Chinese who don't even know the game was played?" You gotta love McKay.

## October 14, 1967:
## USC 24–ND 7 (Notre Dame), 59,075

It didn't take long for John McKay to exact revenge. It would be six years before Notre Dame would beat USC again. It was easy to see why the

STREET and SMITH'S Official Yearbook

COLLEGE 1967 *Football*

60 CENTS

MOST COMPLETE · MOST INFORMATIVE

RON DRAKE
Univ. of
Southern
California

Schedules

Selectors' Chart

MID-WEST
BIG TEN
MID AMERICAN
OHIO
By Paul Hornung

THE EAST
IVY LEAGUE
YANKEE • MAINE
MIDDLE ATLANTIC
PENN COLL. CONF.
By Tim Horgan

ATLANTIC and SOUTHERN
CAROLINA CONF.
By Jack Horner

SOUTHEASTERN
OHIO VALLEY • GULF
By Tom Siler

SOUTHWEST
LONE STAR • SOUTHLAND
By Jim Trinkle

BIG EIGHT
MISSOURI VALLEY
NO. CENT. • MIAA
By Bob Hurt

WEST. ATH. CONF.
ROCKY MOUNTAIN
By John Mooney

WEST COAST
SO. CALIF. • CALIF. A. A.
FAR WESTERN
By Paul Zimmerman

NORTHWEST
BIG SKY
By Don Zupan
N.W. SMALL COLLEGES
By Carl Cluff

End Ron Drake was on the Trojan team that helped gain revenge for the 1966 slaughter of USC by whipping the Irish, 24–7, in 1967. *Sporting News Archives.*

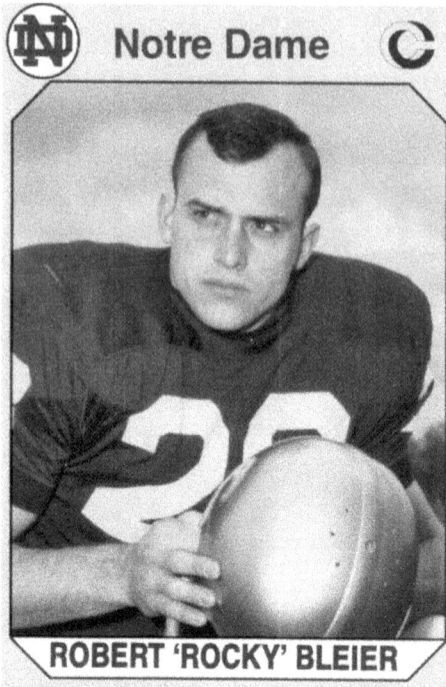

Notre Dame

ROBERT 'ROCKY' BLEIER

Running back Rocky Bleier made a name for himself at Notre Dame from 1965 to 1967, fighting in the Vietnam War and later playing for the Pittsburgh Steelers. His teams lost one game to USC. *Collegiate Collection.*

Notre Dame

TOM SCHOEN

Safety Tom Schoen earned consensus all-American honors in 1967. He helped beat USC two out of three years. *Collegiate Collection.*

1967 team was the first victim: Orenthal James Simpson, the junior college transfer. The first half was no example of great college football. Notre Dame led 7–0 at the half following a 3-yard keeper by quarterback Terry Hanratty. The second half was all O.J., who scored from the 1, the 36 and the 17. And Rikki Aldridge kicked a 22-yard field goal.

"The turning point of the 1967 season was that Notre Dame game," quarterback Steve Sogge recalled, according to Rappoport. "Southern Cal feels it has to beat Notre Dame even though it's a non-conference game. There's a tremendous amount of pride going. Everyone talks about the UCLA game, but I never held UCLA in the same esteem as Notre Dame."

McKay refused to send the Trojans onto the field first and won a battle of bluffs. Parseghian sent the Fighting Irish out first. Whether this game of chess bothered Notre Dame isn't known, but USC intercepted seven passes, four by linebacker Adrian Young, and followed Simpson's running for a 24–7 victory that "gave a national championship season its legs," reported Bisheff and Schrader.

Notre Dame publicist Roger Valdiserri said that he knew what the O.J. stood for: "'O Jesus' as in 'O Jesus, there he goes again.'" The Trojans only lost to Oregon State, 3–0, and they beat Indiana, 14–3, in the Rose Bowl to win John McKay's second national championship. Simpson, Adrian Young, Tim Rossovich and Ron Yary were all-Americans. Notre Dame finished 8-2 with a No. 5 ranking, and it had plenty of its own all-Americans: Tom Schoen, Kevin Hardy, Jim Seymour, Mike McGill, John Pergine, Dick Swatland and Jim Smithberger. Those were the days, my friends.

# November 30, 1968:
## ND 21–USC 21 (L.A. Coliseum), 82,659

The next two years, unfortunately, were like kissing your sister—twice. Notre Dame came into the game 7-2, and USC was 9-0. The tie landed USC No. 4 nationally because Ohio State and Penn State were undefeated, and Texas at 9-1-1 finished ahead of USC, also at 9-1-1. The Irish were No. 5.

So 82,659 people poured into the L.A. Coliseum to see if the Irish could stop O.J. They did. He only gained 55 yards on twenty-one carries. The game started with Sandy Durko intercepting a Joe Theisman pass and romping 21 yards for the score. Ron Ayala converted, and USC led after forty seconds.

O.J. Simpson, probably the greatest back who ever played for USC, rushed for 150 yards and three touchdowns in the Trojans' 1967 victory over the Fighting Irish. *Sporting News Archives.*

But then Notre Dame marched 86 yards, Ron Dushney went over from the three and Scott Hempel kicked the extra point, making it 7–7. But they were not done. Still in the first quarter, halfback Bob Gladieux went 57 yards on a pitchout, and the Irish led, 14–7, after Hempel's conversion. In the second period, Theisman teamed with former quarterback (now halfback) Coley O'Brien to score. Theisman pitched to O'Brien, who threw back to Theisman, who bounced into the end zone. ND led, 21–7, at halftime.

USC had to make some adjustments, and it did. Since O.J. was having a hard time, quarterback Steve Sogge started faking to him and throwing. Then Simpson finished off a 65-yard drive with a TD. Next, Gerry Shaw intercepted a Theisman pass and went to the USC 46. It didn't take long for Sogge to find Sam Dickerson on the goal line, and the score was tied, 21–21.

Neither team was able to break the tie—Notre Dame muffed two field goals, and Sogge failed to complete a critical pass. Nobody was happy with the tie, but it was better than a loss.

## October 18, 1969:
## USC 14–ND 14 (Notre Dame), 59,075

This was getting old. With two coaches the caliber of McKay and Parseghian, both teams were always in the hunt. The year 1969 was no different. USC finished at 9-0-1 and a No. 3 ranking. The Irish were relegated to No. 5, finishing 8-2-1.

The Irish were so tough defensively that they were able to hold USC's great running back Clarence Davis to 75 yards. Nobody scored in the first half, but Theisman got the Irish going in the third quarter with a 74-yard drive in eleven plays. Bill Barz dove over from the one, and ND led, 7–0. Then USC came back with quarterback Jimmy Jones leading the team 75 yards to a score. The TD was the result of a 19-yard pass from Jones, making it 7–7. Going into the fourth quarter, Tyrone Hudson intercepted a Theisman pass and returned it to the Irish 15. Then Jones threw to Dickerson for another score, and the Trojans were ahead, 14–7. Then USC had to punt from its own 3, but big Mike McCoy, blocking the punt with his jaw, saved the day. Walt Patulski recovered on the seven, Denny Allen scored the touchdown and the score was tied once more. With two minutes left, Hempel tried a 31-yard field goal for ND, and the ball hit the crossbar. "God was a Trojan on that kick," McKay said.

## November 28, 1970:
## USC 38–ND 28 (L.A. Coliseum), 64,694

In five more games against McKay, Ara only won once. That's funny because in that period, Ara went 47-8 and won one national championship, while McKay was 43-11-4 and won two national championships. They dominated football from 1972 to 1974. USC was either winning championships or spoiling Notre Dame's chances. In 1970, Notre Dame came to town undefeated, ranking No. 1, and went home losers, 38–28. The Trojans were 5-4-1, their worst season since 1961. It didn't matter.

Notre Dame took the opening kickoff and marched 80 yards, and Theisman went over for the score from 25 out. Hempel converted. Trojan fans expected

Quarterback Joe Theismann never won the Heisman, but it wasn't for want of trying. An all-American in 1970, Joe was on teams that lost only four games in three years. *Collegiate Collection.*

that, but not what happened next. Quarterback Jimmy Jones guided USC to three straight touchdowns. Davis scored on a 3-yard run, and Ayala converted, making it 7–7. The Trojans made a first down on the ND 5, and Davis carried it in for the score. Ayala missed the kick. Then Jones hit end Sam Dickerson with a 45-yard touchdown, with the ball bouncing off ND's Clarence Ellis first and into Sam's hands. Jones threw to Bobby Chandler for the two-point conversion. It was 21–14 at the half. It was pouring rain, and Theisman had an incredible day: 33 of 55 passes for 528 yards.

In the second half, Irish's Darryl Dewan fumbled, and Ken Carter recovered on the Notre Dame 17. Three plays later, Mike Berry ran it in from the one but fumbled in the end zone. However, Pete Adams recovered the ball for a touchdown. The kick was good. A few minutes later, Theisman was forced back into his own end zone, where he fumbled. It was recovered by tackle John Vella, and the Trojans led, 38–14. Then Theisman threw a 46-yard pass to Larry Parker for a touchdown. This was followed by Theisman scoring on a 1-yard run after a 69-yard drive. The game ended that way, 38–28, and the Irish dream of an undefeated season was down the drain.

Ara Parseghian was upset. Who expected this from USC after it had lost to UCLA the previous week, 45–20? For the fourth time in forty years, a Notre Dame team was beaten out of a national championship by the Trojans. The Irish finished No. 2 in the national rankings while USC was No. 15 at 6-4-1.

## October 23, 1971:
## USC 28–ND 14 (Notre Dame), 59,075

Things didn't get any better in 1971 for Notre Dame. USC came to town 2-4, while the Irish had a 5-0 record. Never mind. The Trojans took it to them again, winning 28–14. The Irish had allowed 16 points the entire season and had not had a TD scored against them for fourteen quarters. Forget it. USC took care of that. The credit goes to a pregame talk by McKay, said Applegate in his book.

"We've been disgraceful this season," he said, "and it's a crime. If we're going to play this game, let's play it as well as we can…forget about yourself and play as a team, as men, and if you don't, it may be the last goddamn time some of you may ever get a chance to play—if I have to play nobody."

USC charged out of the locker room and tore Notre Dame apart. Defensive end Glenn Byrd intercepted a pass by Cliff Brown and returned it to the ND 48. Jones threw to Edsel Garrison on the 3, and he scored. Mike Rae kicked the extra point, making it 7–0. Notre Dame answered. Halfback Gary Diminick returned the kickoff 66 yards. Notre Dame pushed down to the 3, and Andy Huff took the ball in for the score. Bob Thomas converted.

Then it was USC's turn. Charlie Hinton returned the kickoff 65 yards to the ND 35. Mike Rae threw a TD pass to Edsel in the end zone and then kicked the extra point, making it 14–7 USC at the end of the first quarter. Then Jones completed a 42-yard pass to Sam Cunningham, and Sam the Bam went over from the 1, making it 21–7. Then Larry Dyer intercepted a ND pass and raced 53 yards for another touchdown. Notre Dame closed out the scoring when John Cieszkowlski ran it in from the 4. Thomas kicked the extra point, and the game ended 28–14.

"I was trying to pull two guys apart when I felt someone kick me right in the butt," said USC assistant Craig Fertig, according to Rappoport. "I turned around and saw it was the Notre Dame leprechaun. He ran up into the stands, and I sure wasn't going to chase him into that crowd."

Well, it wasn't so bad. The Irish had their butts kicked by LSU to end the season 8-2 and a No. 13 ranking. USC finished 6-4-1 but still managed No. 20 in the polls.

## December 2, 1972:
## USC 45–ND 23 (L.A. Coliseum), 75,243

Things improved "slightly" for USC in 1972, since they won the national championship with a team that many consider to be the best college squad of all time. The team, believe it or not, included offensive tackle Pete Adams; fullback Sam Cunningham; tailbacks Anthony Davis, Manfred Moore and Rod McNeil; split ends Edsel Garrison and John McKay Jr.; quarterbacks Pat Haden and Mike Rae; defensive backs Artimus Parker and Charles Hinton; wide receiver Lynn Swann; and linebacker Richard Wood. Not too shabby. ND, meanwhile, was going 8-3, while USC finished 12-0 with its closest game a 30–21 win over Stanford. "Southern Cal taught us speed was everything," said Tom Pagna. "I think Bear Bryant was the first to say it."

It was a disaster for the Irish. On the kickoff, Davis rambled 97 yards for a touchdown, but ND's Greg Marx blocked the point after. The Irish, led by sophomore quarterback Tom Clements, came right back, and Bob Thomas kicked a 45-yard field goal, making it 6–3. Then it was USC's turn. Following a pass interference penalty against Swann, Davis rushed over from the one and Rae converted, and the score was 13–3. Davis scored his third touchdown in the first quarter following an Eric Penick fumble on the Irish 9-yard line. Clements took the Irish on a 73-yard drive to make the score 19–10 at halftime.

In the second half, ND charged on the field, but a Clements pass was intercepted by Chuck Hinton. The drive was capped by a 4-yard TD run by Davis, and the score was 25–10 after a two-point conversion failed. Then Mike Townsend intercepted a Rae pass, and Clements took the Irish down to the eleven, where he hit Diminick in the end zone. The point after was good, and the score was 25–17. But then Townsend intercepted another pass, and Clements marched the Irish down the field and threw a TD pass from the ten to Mike Creany. The score was now 25–23, but that was it for the Irish. USC scored 20 more points. Davis had another kickoff return for a TD—95 yards—and scored on an 8-yard run, and Cunningham finished things off with a 1-yard plunge. The final score was

STREET and SMITH'S OFFICIAL Yearbook
COLLEGE 1972 *Football* 75¢
MOST COMPLETE · MOST INFORMATIVE

PETE ADAMS
Southern California

Schedules
Selectors' Chart

MID-WEST
BIG TEN
MID AMERICAN
OHIO
By Paul Hornung

THE EAST
IVY LEAGUE
YANKEE
MIDDLE ATLANTIC
PENNSYLVANIA CONF.
By Tom Ascenzia

ATLANTIC and
SOUTHERN
CAROLINA CONF
CENTRAL INT. A.A.
MIDEAST · SWAC
By Smith Barrier

SOUTHEASTERN
OHIO VALLEY
GULF SOUTH
By Tom Siler

SOUTHWEST
LONE STAR · SOUTHLAND
By Jim Trinkle

BIG EIGHT
MISSOURI VALLEY
NO. CENTRAL
By Del Black

WEST. ATH. CONF.
ROCKY MOUNTAIN
By John Mooney

PACIFIC EIGHT
SO. CALIF · CALIF A.A.
FAR WESTERN
PACIFIC COAST A.A.
By Dwight Chapin

NORTHWEST
BIG SKY
By Jeff Herman

All-American Pete Adams was an important offensive lineman in the USC surge against Notre Dame in 1972. The Trojans won, 45–23, thanks to the heroics of Mike Rae, Lynn Swann and Anthony Davis. *Sporting News Archives.*

45–23. USC proceeded to dismantle Ohio State in the Rose Bowl, 42–17, and earned a No. 1 ranking.

"These superb young warriors won the national championship in a barrage of ballots," Rappoport wrote. "The Trojans became the first college football team in history to capture every first place ballot from the voters in the United Press International and Associated Press polls." Notre Dame settled for No. 14 after being killed by Nebraska in the Orange Bowl, 40–6.

**DAVE CASPER**

Tight end Dave Casper was one of the greatest players to suit up for the Fighting Irish. He won academic and consensus all-American honors in 1973. Casper teams only beat USC once, but his presence was always felt. *Collegiate Collection.*

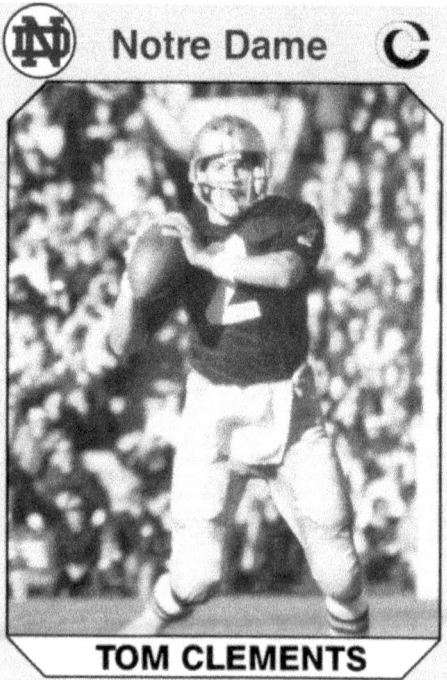

**TOM CLEMENTS**

Quarterback Tom Clements led the Irish to the national championship in 1973. He had a 54.1 percentage and twenty-four touchdowns at Notre Dame. *Collegiate Collection.*

## October 27, 1973:
## ND 23–USC 14 (Notre Dame), 50,075

Now it was Ara's turn. Winning eleven straight and outscoring opponents 358–66 in the regular season, Parseghian had his second national championship. USC meanwhile, was merely 9-1-1, settling for eighth place in the final polls. But USC came into South Bend 5-0-1 with running back Anthony Davis primed. It didn't matter. Irish running back Eric Penick was the hero of the day, gaining 118 yards—50 more than the entire USC team—as well as an 85-yard touchdown run that broke the Trojans' backs.

"I was psyched up when I went on the field and I'm still psyched," Penick said in Bisheff and Schrader's book. "I'll probably be psyched until the day I die."

Bob Thomas kicked three field goals, and the Irish went home victorious, 23–14. Notre Dame went into the Sugar Bowl ranked only third, but a thrilling 24–23 victory over Alabama made the team No. 1. That team included tight end Dave Casper, quarterback Clements, split end Pete Demmerle, guard Gerry DiNardo and defensive backs Tim Rudnick and Mike Townsend. USC settled for eighth place in the final polls.

## November 30, 1974:
## USC 55–ND 24 (L.A. Coliseum), 83,552

Now it was USC's turn again. This was getting old. The Coaches Poll made USC No. 1 (Oklahoma was on probation), even after losing the opening game of the season to Arkansas, 20–7, and later being tied by California. The Irish, meanwhile, were only 10-2 and finished ranked sixth, having lost to Purdue and USC. The only problem was that the USC loss was the last game of the season, and the Irish were destroyed, 55–24. I remember this game well. In 1972, Anthony Davis had scored six touchdowns in the first meeting with ND. In 1973, he was held in check, but anything could happen in 1974, and it did.

Notre Dame came out strong and moved to a 24–0 lead in the first half. Then Davis scored on a lateral from Pat Haden just before the half ended. When the third quarter started, he took the opening kickoff 102 yards for a touchdown, and USC never looked back, scoring 35 points in the quarter.

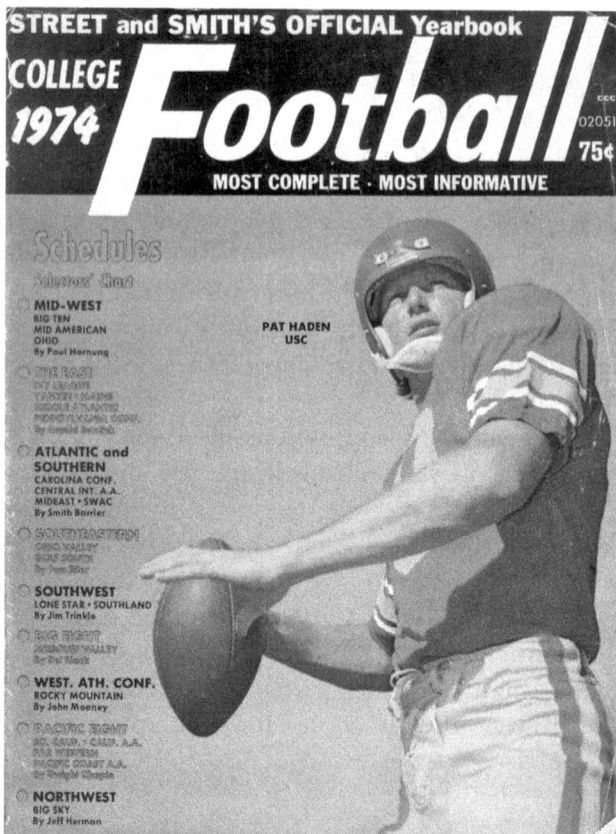

*Left*: Pat Haden, current athletic director at USC, was one of the Trojans' most popular and successful quarterbacks of all time. He led USC to two national championships in 1972 and 1974 and helped beat the Irish two times in his career. *Sporting News Archives.*

*Below*: The 1974 skirmish was famous for one player, running back Anthony Davis. After being down 24–6 in the first half, USC, behind Davis, scored 28 points in nine minutes, and the game ended 55–24. *ND Archives.*

Haden orchestrated the win, with Davis also tallying on a 6-yard run and a 4-yard dash. (Davis was inducted into the College Football Hall of Fame in 2005.) So, USC polished off Ohio State in the Rose Bowl and ended up No. 1 in the nation. Parseghian announced that he was retiring after the Orange Bowl game against Alabama. He had simply had enough. He went to the bowl game and promptly beat the No. 1 team in the nation, Alabama, 13–11. Ara Parseghian, one of the greatest coaches in college history, led his team to No. 6 in the final polls. He went out in style but not to the delight of the Irish faithful.

# DAN DEVINE (0-1) VS. JOHN MCKAY (1-0), 1975

## October 25, 1975:
## USC 24–ND 17 (Notre Dame), 59,075

Ara Parseghian said that when he told Notre Dame he was going to retire after the Alabama game, Father Edmund P. Joyce replied that his replacement had already been hired: Dan Devine of Missouri. Devine had been a finalist ten years earlier when Ara was hired. He coached the Irish for six seasons, compiling a 53-16-1 record. In his first year, he had to face a legend, John McKay, who also was in his final year. Notre Dame had to play USC with a 5-1 record. Meanwhile, McKay was 6-0, but USC had lost their last four games of the season. A 20–0 win in the Liberty Bowl salvaged the season and earned a No. 17 ranking. The Irish finished at 8-3 with no ranking. McKay resigned from USC to become head man with the new Tampa Bay Bucs, apparently because of a fivefold salary increase and the chance to build a team from the ground up.

The Notre Dame game on October 25, 1975, featured some outstanding Irish athletes: split ends Ted Burgmeier and Kris Haines, right guard Ernie Hughes, tight end Ken MacAfee, left half Al Hunter, fullback Jerome Heavens, defensive end Ross Browner, right end Willie Fry, middle linebacker Bob Golic, defensive back Luther Bradley and a defensive end named Rudy Ruettinger (think of the film *Rudy*). Some of these guys would be around for Devine's 1977 championship team. Meanwhile, USC had quarterback Vince Evans, a great running back in Ricky Bell, guard Donnie Hickman,

Tackle Steve Niehaus, who played from 1972 to 1975, was a unanimous all-American defensive player in 1975. Unfortunately, his teams lost four straight to USC. *Collegiate Collection.*

defensive end Gary Jeter, linebackers Rod Martin and Clay Matthews, offensive tackle Marvin Powell, fullback Mosi Tatupu and defensive back Dennis Thurman. It was enough.

# DAN DEVINE (1-4) VS. JOHN ROBINSON (4-1), 1976–1980

## November 27, 1976:
## USC 17–ND 13 (L.A. Coliseum), 76,561

Dan Devine didn't fare any better against John Robinson than McKay. He faced him five times and lost four. Robinson, another Oregon product, took

Ricky Bell, who was on teams that beat Notre Dame three times in a row, 1974–76, averaged 5.2 yards per carry during his career at USC. Bell died of a muscle inflammation disease at twenty-nine. *Sporting News Archives.*

over for McKay, who headed to Florida. Devine, who went 9-3, was 8-2 when they faced the Trojans. USC, meanwhile, didn't lose another game the rest of the season after the first one, ending up 11-1 and ranked No. 2, while the Irish ended up ranked No. 12.

Notre Dame went into this game 8-2, but the most significant point of the season was that a guy named Joe (Montana), now a sophomore, injured his shoulder and didn't play the entire year.

## October 22, 1977:
## ND 49–USC 19 (Notre Dame), 59,075

The year 1977 was a remarkable one for Notre Dame but not so much USC, which was 5-1 when it played the Irish but finished the season ranked No. 13 at 8-4. Notre Dame was a different story. After losing to Mississippi in the second game of the season, a fortuitous thing happened in the Purdue game, even though it was not fortunate for starting quarterback Gary Forystek, who was seriously injured. He was replaced by Rusty Lisch, who in turn was replaced by Joe Montana, with Purdue leading 24–14 with eleven minutes remaining. Joe led the Irish to a 31–24 victory, and a legend was launched. Devine made Joe the starting quarterback, and Notre Dame went on to win its remaining nine games, earning the national championship.

One of those games was on October 22, when USC faced the Irish at Notre Dame Stadium. Coach Dan Devine had a surprise for his men and for USC. When they returned to the locker room after warm-ups, each player found a green jersey at his place. Dressed in the new garb, the team went out, put the stadium into a virtual frenzy and proceeded to undress USC, 49–19.

Montana led the team to a quick score, but USC linebacker Mario Celloto recovered a fumble and scored from 5 yards out. After several missed field goals, Joe led the team to twenty-eight unanswered points, including two touchdown passes to all-American end Ken MacAfee. A wide receiver and defensive back, Ted Burgmeier came into his own in this game. He intercepted a pass to set up a TD, ran 21 yards on a fake field goal to lead to another touchdown and passed to Tom Domin for a two-point conversion after a bobbled snap from center. USC could not score until the fourth quarter, when it was a little late. Chalk one up for the leprechaun.

## Notre Dame

**ROSS BROWNER**

*Left*: Ross Browner, defensive end, was also one of the greatest players ever to put on a Notre Dame uniform. He polished off his career in 1977 with a 49–19 win over USC. *Collegiate Collection*.

*Below*: Dan Devine broke out the green jerseys in 1977 and promptly broke the Trojans' hearts with a dominating 49–19 victory that, coupled with a 38–10 win over Texas in the Cotton Bowl, gave Notre Dame its tenth national championship. *ND Archives*.

## November 25, 1978:
## USC 27–ND 25 (L.A. Coliseum), 84,256

Notre Dame had visions of repeating its 1977 championship, while USC had dreams of its own. The Irish still had Joe Montana, so anything was possible, and they went into USC-ND game 8-2. Unfortunately, they had lost the first two games of the year to Missouri and Michigan, but they righted the ship—until they played USC, that is. The Trojans, meanwhile, went into the game 9-1, having lost only to Arizona State.

USC took control of the game right away, marching to a 24–6 lead behind the likes of Marcus Allen, Ronnie Lott, Charles White, Anthony Munoz and Paul MacDonald. However, Montana put everything together in the fourth quarter and led an incredible comeback. He hit Kris Haines with a 57-yard touchdown pass. Then he led the Irish on a 98-yard drive, ending with a 1-yard plunge by fullback Pete Buchanan. The Irish defense held, and Notre Dame got the ball back with one minute and thirty-five seconds to play. Montana led another drive, which culminated with a 2-yard scoring pass to Pete Holohan to put the Irish ahead, 25–24. Unfortunately, he left forty-five seconds on the clock. That was enough for quarterback Paul MacDonald to lead the Trojans with a 35-yard pass to Calvin Sweeney. With four seconds left on the clock, Frank Jordan kicked a 37-yard field goal, and the Trojans won. Montana extended his comeback mastery in the Cotton Bowl with a last-minute win over Houston, 35–34. But USC was even better, beating Michigan, 17–3, in the Rose Bowl to claim Robinson's only national championship. The Irish finished seventh.

## October 20, 1979:
## USC 42–ND 23 (Notre Dame), 59,075

The year 1979 was a down year for Notre Dame. The team finished 7-4, out of the national picture. USC, however, was up to its usual tricks and finished 11-0-1 and No. 2 nationally. (The only reason it did not take the first spot is because Alabama went 12-0, but I doubt if 'Bama was any better.) USC's "leftovers"—like Allen, Lott, White and Munoz—were augmented by linebacker Chip Banks, safety Joey Browner, offensive guard Brad Budde and offensive tackle Bruce Matthews. Of course, Notre Dame wasn't

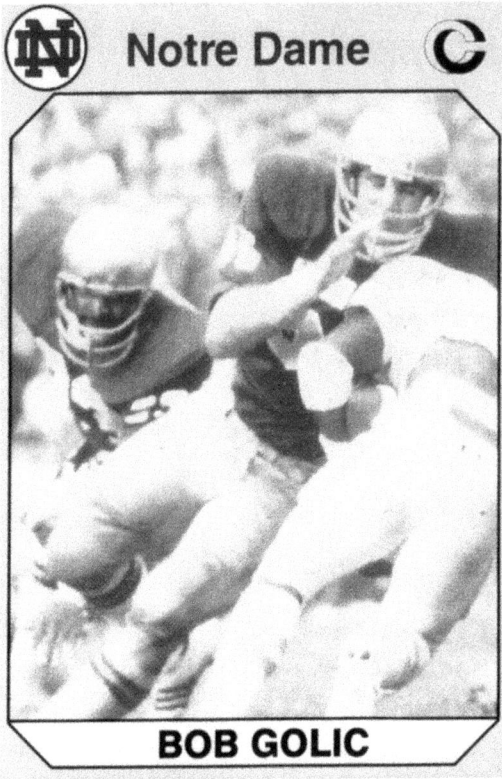

# Notre Dame

## BOB GOLIC

*Left*: Linebacker Bob Golic, who played from 1975 to 1978, was a two-time all-American and helped win the national championship in 1977. He finished 1-3 against the Trojans. *Collegiate Collection.*

*Below*: Joe Montana almost rescued Notre Dame in this 1978 classic, which USC won, 27–25. Down 24–6, Montana rallied the Irish to a 25–24 lead but left enough time for Frank Jordan to kick a game-winning field goal that led to USC's national championship. *ND Archives.*

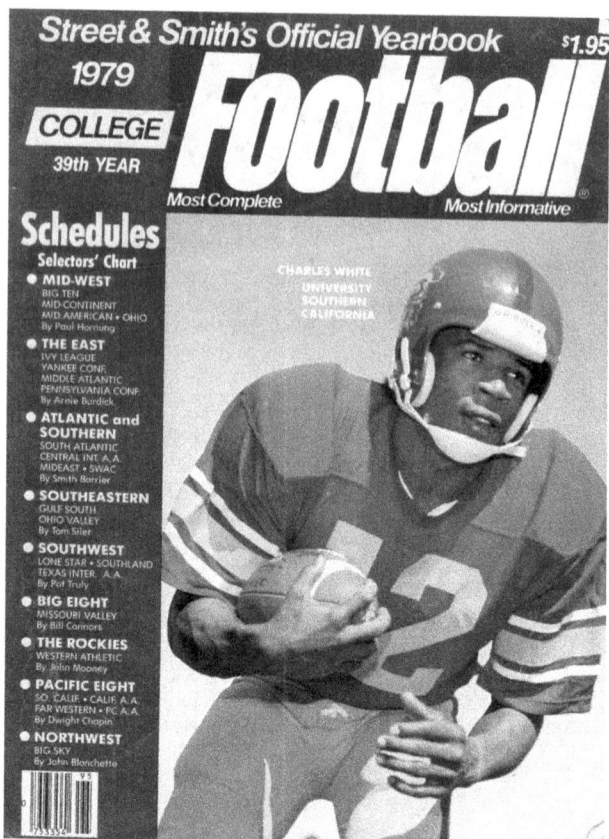

Charles White, Heisman Trophy winner in 1979, gained 261 yards on forty-four carries to help defeat Notre Dame. *Sporting News Archives.*

chopped liver, since its cast featured linebacker Bob Crable, safety Dave Duerson, running back Vagas Ferguson, flanker Pete Hollohan, guard Tim Huffman, center John Scully and cornerback Dave Waymer.

It was the sixth game on the Irish schedule, and the two really slugged it out, with more than 500 yards each, but nobody dominated more than running back Charles White, who gained 261 yards rushing on forty-four carries. USC won.

Robinson was always the first one to celebrate White's toughness on the field. "He was running down the field," Robinson recalled in *Fight On!,* "and three Notre Dame guys come flying over to knock him out of bounds...He turns right into them, and bodies go flying all over the place. Who's the first guy to jump up? Yeah, Charlie was the man." White also had 135 yards as sophomore and 205 as a junior against the Irish. ND was happy to see him graduate.

## The Games

### December 6, 1980:
### USC 20–ND 3 (L.A. Coliseum), 82,663

The year 1980 wasn't a bad one for either team, as Notre Dame finished 9-2-1 and USC 8-2-1. The Irish finished ninth and USC eleventh in the final polls. Notre Dame had 9 wins and only 1 tie going into the game in Los Angeles, while USC was 7-2-1. As usual, the past meant nothing, as USC dominated for a 20–3 victory and its third win in a row. The offense was led by Allen (still), offensive tackle Keith Van Horne, offensive guard Bruce Matthews and offensive tackle Don Mosebar, while the defense featured defensive back Ronnie Lott, linebacker Chip Banks and safety Joey Browner. Notre Dame had equal talent: running back Phil Carter, wide receiver Pete Holohan, quarterback Blair Kiel and tight end Dean Masztak on offense and cornerback Chris Brown, linebacker Bob Crable, safety Dave Duerson and defensive end Scott Zettek on defense.

The loss also led to a Notre Dame defeat to Georgia in the Sugar Bowl, 17–10. Thanks to USC, Notre Dame had its national chances smashed. It also marked the end of the Devine era at Notre Dame. He announced on August 15, 1980, that he would be leaving Notre Dame at the end of the season to spend more time with his wife. He moved back to Arizona and died on May 9, 2002, about two years after his wife.

# GERRY FAUST (0-2) VS. JOHN ROBINSON (2-0), 1981–1982

### October 24, 1981:
### USC 14–ND 7 (Notre Dame), 59,075

When Gerry Faust was selected to succeed Dan Devine as coach of Notre Dame in 1981, it was the signal of five years of mediocrity. Faust was apparently chosen because Moeller High School in Cincinnati, where he coached, constantly fed superior athletes to Notre Dame, because he loved Notre Dame and because he was such a nice guy that the administration wanted to give him a chance. Big mistake.

His first year, he went 5-6 (not disastrous), with a 20–7 win over Michigan State, a 38–0 win over Navy, a 35–3 win over Georgia Tech and a 35–7 win over Air Force. When the Irish met USC on October 24 in South Bend, ND was 2-3. USC was 5-1. Quarterback John Mazur and running back Marcus Allen led USC, while ND was paced by quarterbacks Blair Kiel and Tim Koegel and running back Phil Carter. Allen had his greatest year, winning the Heisman Trophy, setting sixteen NCAA records and becoming the first runner to gain more than 2,000 yards. He won the Walter Campbell and Maxwell Trophies and averaged 212.9 yards per game. USC ended up being ranked No. 14, while Notre Dame didn't even go to a bowl game.

## November 27, 1982:
## USC 17–ND 13 (L.A. Coliseum), 76,459

The year 1982 was remarkable for the resignation of John Robinson. His USC team finished 8-3, certainly very respectable, but Robinson had had enough. "It was like everything else in life," he said in *Fight On!* "Some people in the NFL had talked to me the year before, but that isn't what was behind my decision. I just got caught up with some influential L.A. people who wanted me to be involved in politics. I think that was a big part of it. I was forty-six years old and needed a change."

All-American Jack Del Rio, current defensive coach of the NFL Denver Broncos, played for USC from 1981 to 1984, losing two and winning two against the Irish. He also was a runner-up for the Lombardi Trophy in 1984. *Sporting News Archives.*

So Robinson faced Faust for the final time and, naturally, walked away with another victory. USC was 7-3 going into the game, and ND was 6-3-1—not terrible. Michael Harper of USC scored with a 1-yard run with forty-eight seconds remaining, even though the Irish thought that he had fumbled before he crossed the goal line. Blair Kiel tried to complete a 32-yard pass in the end zone to end the game, but it was knocked down by safety Joey Browner. USC finished No. 15 in the final polls, while Notre Dame, of course, was out of the picture.

# GERRY FAUST (3-0) VS. TED TOLLNER (0-3), 1983–1985

## October 22, 1983:
## ND 27–USC 6 (Notre Dame), 59,075

USC turned to an assistant coach, Ted Tollner (26-20-1), on Robinson's recommendation and later Larry Smith (44-25-3) for the next ten years. They finished 70-45-4, not exactly terrible but certainly not up to the lofty standards USC was used to. The good news was that Faust got to face a Tollner team for the next three years, winning all of the matches. In 1983, the Irish went into the game 4-2 and came out victorious, 27–6. It was their most lopsided win since the 49–19 victory in 1977. In fact, it began a string of 11 straight victories for the Irish, the longest streak ever.

In 1983, Blair Kiel led Notre Dame to 27–6 victory over USC. *ND Archives.*

Faust dug out the green jerseys again and apparently inspired the Irish to victory. Tight end Mark Bavaro, quarterback Blair Kiel, kicker John Carney, defensive tackle Mike Gann and tailback Allen Pinkett led the Irish. USC, in turn, had such players as linebacker Keith Browner, safety Tim MacDonald, fullback Kennedy Pola, linebacker Sherman Ratliff, linebacker Jack Del Rio and tailback Michael Harper.

## November 24, 1984:
## ND 19–USC 7 (L.A. Coliseum), 66,342

Surprisingly, 1984's contest wasn't much of a game. Notre Dame started 6-4 that day, while USC was a solid 8-2 and finished 9-3 but went unranked. It probably didn't help that the Trojans lost in consecutive weeks: 29–10 to UCLA and 19–7 to Notre Dame. The Irish did their usual trick of losing a bowl game—this time the Aloha to SMU, 27–20, while the Trojans beat Ohio State, 18–6, in the Rose Bowl. The Irish players included linebacker Robert Banks, tight end Mark Bavaro, split end Tim Brown, kicker John Carney, nose tackle Eric Dorsey, defensive tackle Mike Gann, linebacker Mike Golic, cornerback Mike Haywood and running back Allan Pinkett. USC had linebacker Sam Anno, tailback Ryan Knight, Safety Tim McDonald, Fullback Kennedy Pola, linebacker Jack Del Rio and quarterback Sean Salisbury. Anyway, Faust seemed to have USC's number.

## October 26, 1985:
## ND 37–USC 3 (Notre Dame), 59,075

The year 1985 was worse. Notre Dame was only 2-3 when it faced USC, and the Trojans were 3-2. The Irish ended up 5-6 and USC 6-6. The game was ridiculous, as ND won, 37–3. It also meant the end for Gerry Faust, who had been skating on thin ice. Notre Dame didn't have a good team, but obviously on this day USC could do nothing right.

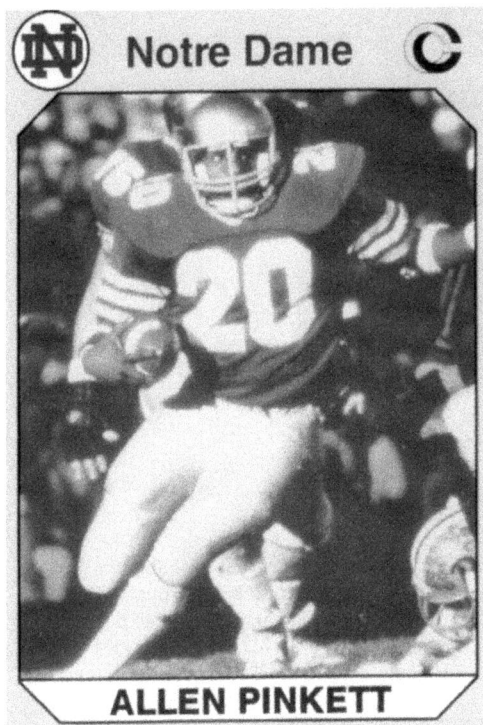

Tailback Allen Pinkett was one of Notre Dame's greatest backs. He rushed for 4,131 yards in his four-year career and helped beat USC three out of four times. *Collegiate Collection.*

# Lou Holtz (1-0) vs. Ted Tollner (0-1), 1986

## November 29, 1986:
## ND 38–USC 37 (L.A. Coliseum), 70,614

Happy days were here again for the Irish. Gerry Faust was gone, and Lou Holtz had arrived. The year 1986 wasn't a great one for the Irish, but it only was a precursor of things to come. Meanwhile, Ted Tollner was facing the inevitable. He finished 7-5 in 1986, but the USC faithful had had enough. It didn't help that Ted had gone 1-7 against some only fair Notre Dame teams and against UCLA in four years.

The 1986 Notre Dame game didn't improve anything. After quarterback Rodney Peete led the Trojans to a 30–12 lead early in the third quarter, ND quarterback Steve Beuerlein was benched for throwing

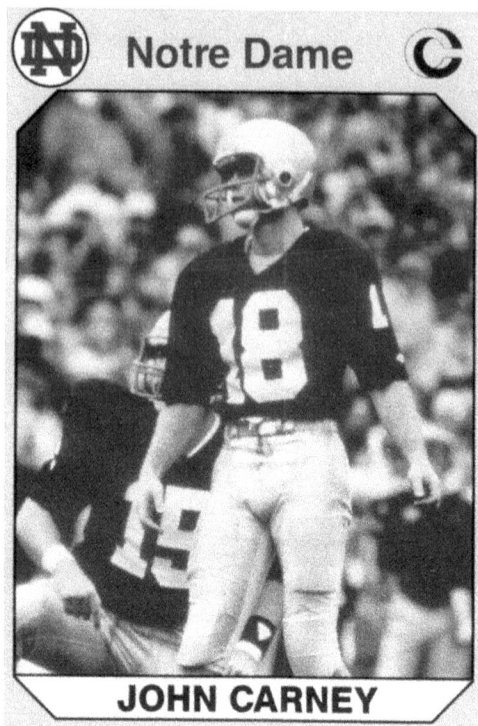

John Carney is probably the greatest kicker to ever come out of Notre Dame. He made twenty out of twenty-five field goals over 40 yards, and he kicked the game winner against USC in 1986. *Collegiate Collection.*

an interception. USC went up 37–20. Holtz reported in his autobiography *Wins, Losses and Lessons* that "Beuerlein came up to me almost in tears. 'Coach, don't let me end my career like this,' Beuerlein said. 'This is my hometown. I am a four-year starter. This is my last game. This is USC. I promise I won't throw another interception.' Then Tim Brown took a kickoff back 56 yards. I said, 'Convince me.'"

Beuerlein went to work. He threw three touchdown passes: 22 yards to Braxton Banks, 43 yards to Milt Jackson and another for 5 yards to Banks to cut the lead to 37–35. It didn't help that Peete was flagged for unsportsmanlike conduct after throwing up his arms when the referees spotted the ball when USC was trying to make a first down. They had to punt, and Tim Brown returned the kick for 56 yards, setting up a 19-yard field goal by John Carney with two seconds left. Tollner had to hear the death knells, as Carney, one of the greatest kickers in football history, nailed the field goal. The Irish went on to Lou's worst season, 5-6, but it didn't matter. The future was beckoning, and USC would not win again until 1996.

# LOU HOLTZ (6-0) VS. LARRY SMITH (0-6), 1987–1992

## October 24, 1987:
## ND 26–USC 15 (Notre Dame), 59,075

Larry Smith was the next fodder for Lou, losing six out of six against the Irish. The new athletic director, Mike McGee, apparently had his own ideas for coach. He hired Larry Smith, the Arizona coach and a close friend. Tollner had no regrets. He said he enjoyed every moment. Now it was time for Smith to suffer—er, enjoy himself as USC football coach. Smith started off with a 4-2 record when he faced Notre Dame. The Irish, meanwhile, had won four out of their first five games. After USC scored an opening touchdown, the Irish unveiled a great running attack, led by Braxton Banks, Ricky Watters and Anthony Johnson, which netted 351 yards rushing and a final 26–15 victory. Notre Dame ended up ranked seventeenth with an 8-4 record, and USC was eighteenth with the same.

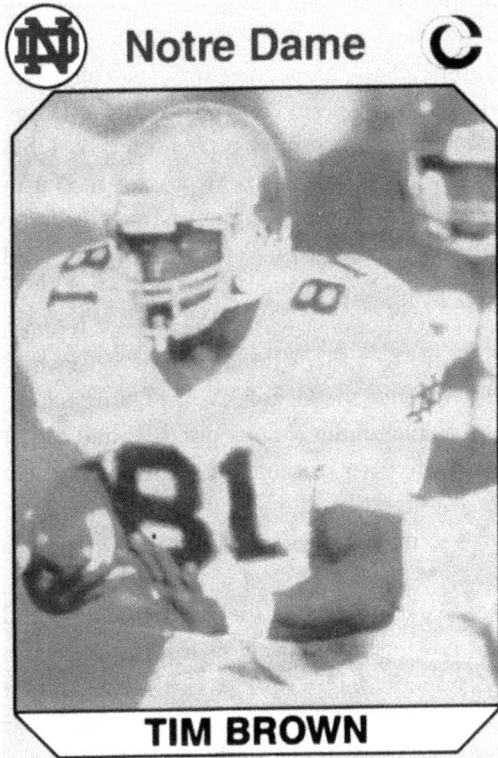

**Notre Dame** ℂ

**TIM BROWN**

Tim Brown, the seventh Notre Dame player to win the Heisman Trophy, had a remarkable career in college and the pros. He helped beat USC four times in a row. *Collegiate Collection.*

# Notre Dame vs. USC

## November 26, 1988:
## ND 27–USC 10 (L.A. Coliseum), 93,829

The year 1988 was one of the greatest years that Notre Dame ever had, and that's saying something. The Irish finished 12-0, with a 19–17 win over Michigan in the first game of the year, a 31–30 barnburner over Miami in the middle and a 27–10 dismantling of USC at the end. Three of the teams they beat finished in the top ten. In fact, USC was also undefeated when it met at the Coliseum in "another game of the century." Not only was USC favored, two of Notre Dame's star running backs, Ricky Watters and Tony Brooks, had been sent home for disciplinary reasons.

The night before the game was a precursor to what would happen on the field, reported Holtz in *The Fighting Spirit*, the story of the 1988 season: "Frank Stams [defensive end] stood up at the back of the room, and he was very emotional and vocal. I don't remember exactly what he said, but it went something like this: 'I don't care what all you guys think. If you're not ready to play this game tomorrow, then I want you just to get the hell out of this room. I don't care if I am the only one on the field, I'm going to play awfully well tomorrow.'" And he did exactly that.

On third and three at the beginning of the game, quarterback Tony Rice faked a pitch to Mark Green and went 65 yards in front of the Notre Dame bench to score. It was the longest run from scrimmage permitted by USC since 1979. On USC's second play from its own 31, Peete passed to Aaron Emanuel, who lost the ball to George Williams. Stams recovered at the Trojan 19. Mark Green went in from the 2-yard line four plays later, and Notre Dame led, 14-0.

In the second period, the Trojans executed a 66-yard drive in eleven plays, featuring a 26-yard throw from Peete to Erik Affholter. Scott Lockwood scored from the one to make it 14–7. After the kickoff, Notre Dame had to punt after three plays, and USC was beginning to look good. It had a first down on the Notre Dame 49 with fifty-two seconds left. But when Peete tried to pass to John Jackson, Jackson slipped and Stan Smagala came up to intercept the ball and race 64 yards to make it 20–7 at halftime. (Reggie Ho missed the extra point.)

Notre Dame was halted on its first two tries in the third period. USC mounted a nice drive, with Peete passing to Leroy Holt for 11 yards and Jackson for 16, as well as runs by Emanuel for 10 and 21 yards. USC had a first down on the four, but the Notre Dame defense and a penalty prompted Quin Rodriguez to kick a 26-yard field goal. Then Notre Dame went on a

70-yard drive, with Mark Green diving over from the one for the score. A 23-yard screen pass reception from Anthony Johnson to the USC 13 was the big gainer. The final score was 27–10. Notre Dame made the perfect season complete with a 34–21 win of West Virginia in the Fiesta Bowl. USC lost to Michigan in the Rose Bowl but ended up 10-2, ranked seventh in the country.

## October 21, 1989:
## ND 28–USC 24 (Notre Dame), 59,075

The Notre Dame fans were getting spoiled under Holtz. This time, the team went 11-0 before losing to Miami in the twelfth game of the season, 27–10. However, ND bounced back to beat Colorado in the Orange Bowl, 21–6, and finish No. 2 in the nation. USC, in the meantime, was recovering after losing to Illinois (Illinois?) in the opening game, 14–13. But then it was 5-1 when it faced the Irish and ended the season 9-2-1, having tied UCLA but

Notre Dame came into the 1989 game on an eighteen-game winning streak and promptly fell behind, 17–7, at the half. However, Tony Rice rallied the Irish to a 28–24 win. *ND Archives.*

having beaten Michigan in the Rose Bowl. USC settled for a No. 8 ranking in the final polls.

The 1989 game was a big deal because Notre Dame was undefeated and ranked No. 1. A brawl in the tunnel before the game marred the contest at ND Stadium, but USC came out strong. Beleaguered quarterback Todd Marinkovich completed 33 of 55 passes and gave the Trojans a 17-7 lead at halftime. But the Irish outscored them, 21-7, in the second half. Tony Rice brought the Irish back and scored on a 5-yard keeper to make the final score 28-24 and keep the Notre Dame streak alive.

## November 24, 1990:
## ND 10–USC 6 (L.A. Coliseum), 91,639

The year 1990 was down for Holtz as he only finished 9-3, with a loss to Colorado in the Orange Bowl, 10-9. This was still good enough for a sixth ranking in the final polls. The Irish were in good shape with an 8-2 record when they faced USC at the Coliseum. About ninety-two thousand people turned out even though USC was only 8-2-1 (it finished 8-4-1, with a loss in the John Hancock Bowl to Michigan State, 17-16, and No. 20 in the polls).

The game wasn't much as the Irish settled for a 10-6 win. It was a remarkable year for Raghib "Rocket" Ismail, who finished second in the Heisman Trophy race and later signed a record contract with the Canadian Football League.

## October 26, 1991:
## ND 34–USC 20 (Notre Dame), 59,075

Notre Dame and Lou Holtz continued their great run, finishing 10-3 with a 39-28 win over Florida State in the Sugar Bowl and a ranking at No. 13 in the final polls. USC had one of its worst years. It was 3-3 when it faced the Irish, but it ended up losing the last six games of the year and finishing 3-8.

In the Notre Dame game, the Trojans, remarkably, had one of their best games of the year, only losing 24-20—in South Bend, no less. But the Irish were loaded; their roster included fullback Jerome Bettis, quarterback Rick Mirer, tailbacks Lee Becton and Reggie Brooks, linebacker Demetrius Dubose, tackle Jim Flanigan, tight end Derek Brown, wide receiver Lake Dawson, kicker Craig Hentrich, offensive guard Mirko Jurkovic, center Tim Ruddy and tight end Irv Smith. The mystery is how they ever lost three games.

## November 28, 1992:
## ND 31–USC 23 (L.A. Coliseum), 90,063

The year 1992 was another great one for the Irish and for Holtz. Rick Mirer was still quarterback, and the Irish were at 10-1-1, with only a tie to Michigan Stare, a loss to Stanford and a 28–3 win over Texas A&M in the Cotton Bowl. They finished fourth in the final poll. USC was 6-3-1 when it faced the Irish, and it finished 6-5-1 It also was the finish of Coach Larry Smith, who was ousted to make room for the return of John Robinson. After getting beat by Fresno State, 24–7, in the Freedom Bowl, Smith said, "Names and logos don't mean anything. You don't beat someone just because of your name and logo." Shortly after that loss and comment, Smith was dismissed.

As for the 1992 game, the Irish won again, 31–23, but it was relatively close. It seemed like USC had lot of talent from six-foot-eight offensive tackle Tony Boselli and six-foot-seven Norberto Garrido to quarterback Rob Johnson and wide receiver Johnnie Morton. The Irish still had Mirer, Bettis, Brooks, Lake Dawson and Irv Smith.

# Lou Holtz (3-1) vs. John Robinson (1-3), 1993–1996

## October 23, 1993:
## ND 31–USC 13 (Notre Dame), 59,075

So 1993 marked the return of one of USC's more successful football coaches who wasn't named McKay or Carroll. John Robinson, who had success in the NFL coaching the Los Angeles Rams, was ready to come back. "I'll find someone who can carry the ball thirty times a game," he promised, according to *Fight On!* "I'm going to put up a stand right where those other Heisman Trophies sit, and I'm going to get somebody to fill it."

Well, he had only fair success in his return trip, finishing 37-21-2, but hail to the victor: he beat Notre Dame twice, lost twice and tied once. He did stop the losing streak with a tie in 1994 and a win 1996. Other than that, it was another ordinary five years.

Things started off in 1993 with a wonderful Notre Dame team squashing USC, 31–13, at South Bend. The Irish went on to beat Florida State, 31–24, and Texas A&M in the Cotton Bowl. In one of the great travesties of justice of all time, Florida State was named No. 1 and the Irish No. 2, even though they both had one loss and the Irish had beaten them. The only mar on Notre Dame's record was a loss to Boston College, 41–39, on a last second field goal. So be it.

The 1993 game was no contest, 31–13.

# November 26, 1994:
# ND 17–USC 17 (L.A. Coliseum), 90,217

The next year, Lou's talent pool diminished, and ND finished 6-5-1. USC was better at 8-3 and managed to tie the Irish, 17–17, and finish the season ranked thirteenth. It might have been like kissing your sister to Holtz, but not to Robinson.

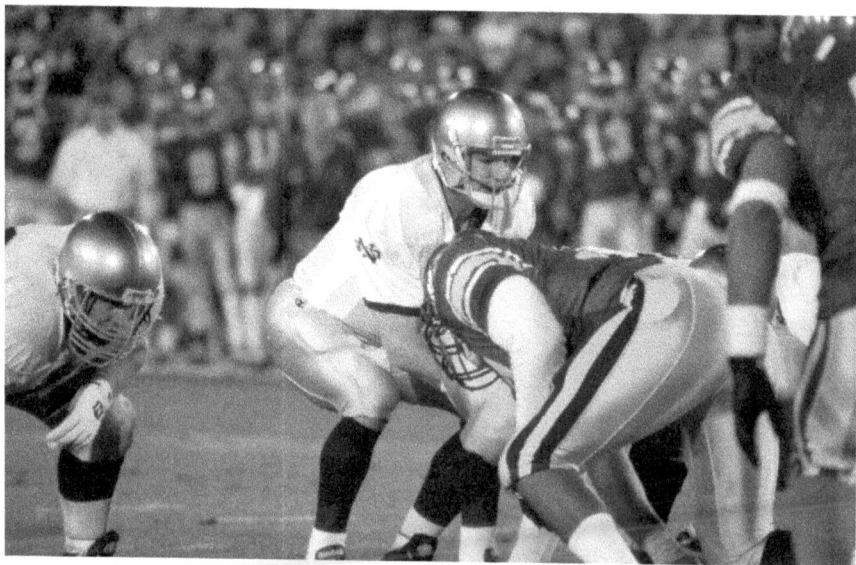

The year 1994 was another nail-biter. USC was 7-3 and Notre Dame 6-4, and the game was even closer, ending in a 17–17 tie. *ND Archives.*

# The Games

## October 21, 1995:
## ND 38–USC 10 (Notre Dame), 59,075

This was the year for USC. It came into the Notre Dame game in South Bend undefeated and ranked No. 5. Meanwhile, the Irish were 5-2, having lost to Northwestern and Ohio State. Never mind, as the Irish took it to them from the beginning. The defense held the Trojans to 10 points, and linebacker Kinnon Tatum forced a USC fumble on the Notre Dame one. USC went on to finish 9-2-1 and win the Rose Bowl, beating Northwestern, 17–3. Robinson continued the Holtz string. Notre Dame finished at No. 11 and USC No. 12.

## November 30, 1996:
## USC 27–ND 20 (L.A. Coliseum), 90,296

The most significant thing about 1996 was the end of Lou Loltz's remarkable eleven years. Was it a coincidence that Leahy, Parseghian and Holtz all coached eleven years? Anyway, Lou finished 100-30-2 (.765), which compares pretty favorably with Leahy's 87-11-9 (.855) and Ara's 95-17-4 (.836). They, of course, were better than everyone else except the master, Knute Rockne (.881). Again, it was a matter of a football coach getting worn out and needing a change. But who would be next?

In 1996, Notre Dame went into the USC game at the end of the year 8-2. The Trojans were 5-6 but ended up winning the game, 27–20. The Irish scored a touchdown to go ahead, 20–12, in the fourth quarter. But USC came back with an eight-play drive, with Delon Washington scoring from 15 yards out. Washington made the two-point conversion, charging into the end zone. Now the score was 20–20, and the game went into overtime. Brad Otton threw a 5-yard touchdown pass to Rodney Sermons, and USC went ahead, 27–20. Mark Cusano knocked down Ron Powlus's fourth-down pass to preserve the victory. USC finished 6-6 but relished this victory. Notre Dame at 8-3 was ranked No. 19 in the final polls.

PASSING GRADES FOR DUCKS & DEVILS • TALENT SHOWS AT ARIZONA & STANFORD

**Street&Smith's College Football**

COLLEGE FOOTBALL

**YEAR OF THE QUARTERBACK**
**Heisman Hopeful Brad Otton Leads USC**

**Huskies' Unfinished Business**

**San Diego State's Back!**

Brad Otton, starting quarterback in 1996, finished his college career completing 410 of 718 passes for 5,359 yards, with forty touchdowns and fourteen interceptions. In 1996, He helped USC beat the Irish, 27–20, throwing the TD pass that won the game. *Sporting News Archives.*

# BOB DAVIE (0-1) VS. JOHN ROBINSON (1-0), 1997

## October 18, 1997:
## USC 20–ND 17 (Notre Dame), 80,225

Years of mediocrity lay ahead for the Fighting Irish. Bob Davie, who had been Holtz's defensive coordinator, was quickly selected to replace the retiring coach. He had twenty years of service as an assistant coach at places like Pittsburgh, Arizona and Texas A&M. He was handsome and well-spoken and seemed a pretty good fit for Notre Dame, but the fans and alumni never seemed to take to Robert, who was anything but rapid. He alienated some by talking about traditions at other schools, and he fired offensive coach Joe Moore, who later sued the university for age discrimination and won. Anyway, Davie finished a decent 3-2 against USC and 35–25 at Notre Dame—not exactly meeting expectations.

In his first year, he finished 7-6, losing to USC, 17–20. He went into the game with 2-4 record. USC was 2-3. These indeed were dog days of football. USC won the game, 20–17, but nobody really seemed to care. It ended up 6-5 for the year, with the Irish 7-6.

# BOB DAVIE (2-1) VS. PAUL HACKETT (1-2), 1998–2000

## November 28 1998:
## USC 10–ND 0 (L.A. Coliseum), 90,096

Davie had a string of eight victories in 1998, having fans dreaming of better days. They had lost their second game to Michigan State but had beaten Michigan, Stanford, Purdue, Boston College and LSU. USC was 7-4, including a 34–17 loss to UCLA. USC coach Robinson quit at the end of the 1997 season following his lackluster second tenure, and Paul Hackett took over as coach. He didn't fare too well either. He won one and lost two to Notre Dame and finished 19-17 before giving up to Pete Carroll.

# Notre Dame vs. USC

Notre Dame was trailing 24–3 in 1999 when a furious rally ended with a miracle recovery by Jabari Holloway of a Jarious Jackson fumble in the end zone. The final score was 25–24 Notre Dame. *ND Archives.*

Notre Dame quarterback Jarious Jackson suffered a severe knee injury at the LSU game and was not available for the USC game. The Trojans took over offensively; the Irish could do nothing and lost, 10–0. USC's Chad Morton rushed for 128 yards. The first touchdown came in the third quarter on a 64-yard drive. Quarterback Carson Palmer threw a 25-yard pass to R. Jay Soward, while runs of 11, 21 and 5 yards by Morton helped moved the ball to the 2-yard line. Palmer then scored the first touchdown of his career on a 2-yard bootleg. With 3:28 left in the quarter, Adam Abrams kicked a 23-yard field goal to complete the scoring.

Notre Dame was pretty pathetic on offense. Arnaz Battle and Eric Chappell completed seven of 22 passes for 94 yards. Rushing leader Autry Denson was held to 46 yards on nineteen carries. Notre Dame finished 9-3, losing to Georgia Tech in the Gator Bowl, while USC finished 8-4, losing in the Sun Bowl to TCU. Neither team was ranked in the top twenty at the end of the year.

# The Games

## October 16, 1999:
## ND 25–USC 24 (Notre Dame), 80,012

The year 1999 was a pretty feeble one for both teams. Notre Dame was 3-3 going into the USC game, while the Trojans were 3-2. This game was one for the ages, though. Notre Dame was trailing 24–3 in the second half after quarterback Mike Van Raaphorst completed twenty-three out of forty-one for 298 yards, and Soward made ten catches for 101 yards. USC was in the driver's seat when David Newbury hit a 29-yard field goal to put USC up 24–3.

Then the Irish went to work. First quarterback Jarious Jackson hit tight end Dan O'Leary with a 7-yard TD pass. On USC's next possession Van Raaphorst fumbled, and Jackson drove the Irish down the field as the rain began to pour. From the USC 17, Jackson scrambled for 13 to the 4-yard line. Donald Driver piled into the end zone from the two, but David Miller missed the extra point and the Trojans led, 24–16, with thirteen minutes left. Next, Miller hit a 33-yard field goal to cut the lead to 25–19.

Then the Irish took over on their own 26-yard line with 6:30 left. Jackson passed to Tony Fisher for 28 yards down the left sideline. After the Irish made to the USC 18, Jackson went back to pass but pulled the ball down and scrambled up the middle to the 1-yard line, where he fumbled into the end zone. Jabari Hollway somehow pounced on the ball and recovered for the Irish TD. A two-point conversion failed, and Notre Dame withstood a final USC gasp to win, 25–24, in their greatest comeback against USC.

Raaphorst summed it up: "We didn't execute on offense. We didn't execute on defense. We didn't execute on special teams." It was the highlight of the year for ND, which finished 5-7, while USC was 6-6.

## November 25, 2000:
## ND 38–USC 21 (L.A. Coliseum), 81,342

The year 2000 saw Notre Dame once more attempt a revival. It went into the USC game 8-2, while the Trojans were a lousy 5-6. Notre Dame was obviously better as Hackett completed his three-year tenure.

Freshman quarterback Matthew LoVecchio ran for two touchdowns and engineered an offense that turned two blocked punts into touchdowns and two interceptions into two more scores. Notre Dame went ahead, 7–0, when Terrence Howard scored on a 1-yard run after a 40-yard drive following a USC blocked punt.

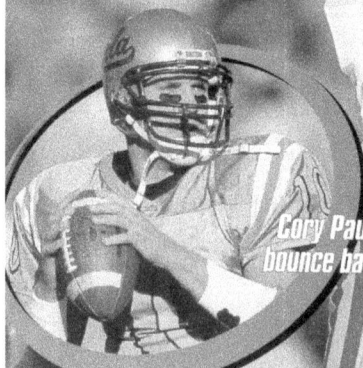

Special Black College Extra ■ The Bowl Glut ■ Chris Simms breaks out

# Street & Smith's

## COLLEGE FOOTBALL 2002

Win a trip to the
HULA BOWL MAUI
2003
ALL-STAR CLASSIC

# Trojan Terror

Southern Cal receiver
Kareem Kelly makes his
bid for All-America

Cory Paus looks to
bounce back at UCLA

$6.99   $7.50 FOREIGN/CANADA
DISPLAY UNTIL OCT. 3RD, '02

Wide receiver Kareem Kelly had a great career at USC from 1999 to 2002. He is second all-time in receiving yards at 3,104. In 2000, he had four catches against ND including a 59-yard TD. *Sporting News Archives.*

USC came back with a 65-yard drive capped by Carson Palmer's 3-yard bootleg to tie the score at 7–7. Then ND's Chad DeBolt blocked a punt by Mike MacGillivray, and Notre Dame went 50 yards, with LoVecchio scoring. Next Tony Driver returned an interception 43 yards to the Trojan 19, where ND eventually scored on a 1-yard run by Fisher, making it 21–7. Then USC got the ball, and Palmer threw a 59-yard TD pass to Kareem Kelly.

In the second half, Glenn Earl intercepted another Palmer pass, and it took Notre Dame five plays for LoVecchio to score again. Palmer threw a 10-yard pass to Antoine Harris, but Notre Dame came back with a 39-yard field goal by Nicholas Setta. After USC stalled, Notre Dame went on an 80-yard drive on the ground, with Julius Jones scoring the last touchdown with 2:57 left. Notre Dame ended the year with a No. 11 ranking in spite of a 41–9 massacre by Oregon State in the Fiesta Bowl. And USC got ready for you know who and its greatest decade of dominance ending in embarrassment.

# BOB DAVIE (1-0) VS. PETE CARROLL (0-1), 2001

## October 20, 2001:
## ND 27–USC 16 (Notre Dame), 80,795

The year 2001 was remarkable for USC. The administration had the wisdom to hire Pete Carroll, even though he was not the first choice. He stayed nine years with the Trojans, accumulating an incredible record, 83-19, and 8-1 against Notre Dame. He didn't have the Irish's number the first year, but he soon got rolling. Bob Davie, who was on his way out himself, managed to go away with a 27–16 win over the Trojans.

It wasn't much of a year for ND or Davie. After losing its first three games, it faced the Trojans with a 2-3 record. USC, meanwhile, wasn't any better under Carroll, with two wins and four losses in a row. The game started off with two touchdowns by USC. Chad Pierson caught a 54-yard pass from Carson Palmer. Then Palmer threw a 20-yard TD pass to Keary Colbert, and the score was 14–0. The Irish scored on a 4-yard run by Terence Howard. After a drive, Notre Dame stopped USC at the one, and the Trojans had to settle for a field goal, making the score 16–10. That was it for USC. Led by quarterback Carlyle Holiday, who scored a TD on a 35-yard run, the Irish outscored the Trojans the rest of the way. Julius Jones scored on a 5-yard run with a little over one minute left. Holiday ran for 98 yards and was nine for twelve passing. Jones rushed for 95 yards.

"This is a very difficult loss because of how much was on the line and how much this game meant to the players and the school," Carroll said. He was to make up for it quickly.

# Tyrone Willingham (0-3) vs. Pete Carroll (3-0), 2002–2004

## November 30, 2002:
## USC 44–ND 13 (L.A. Coliseum), 91,432

While USC was starting an incredible run of victories under Pete Carroll, Notre Dame was having its own troubles going into 2002. George O'Leary, the former Georgia Tech coach, was hired and fired after it was found that he had padded his résumé. So ND turned to its first black coach in history, Tyrone Willingham, a move that pretty well proved to be disastrous. Today, Willingham, a forthright man with an impeccable reputation, is out of football after basically disastrous stints following his success at Stanford. Pete Carroll faced Willingham for three years and helped send him packing with an 0-3 record, 21-15 overall—obviously not good enough for the South Bend alumni.

But strange as it may seem, Willingham got off to a great start, going into the USC game with a 10-1 record. That didn't last long. USC went in with a 9-2 record and was ranked sixth, with Notre Dame seventh. The Trojans absolutely pulverized the Irish. Carson Palmer threw for 425 yards and four touchdowns. USC gained an incredible 610 yards to 109 for the Irish. Strange enough, Notre Dame started with two field goals by Nick Setta, at 34 and 32 yards. Then Mike Williams scored on a 6-yard pass from Palmer. Ryan Kileen converted and then kicked a 22-yard field goal. Then ND's Carlos Pierre-Antoine blocked a punt and recovered it in the end zone. ND actually led, 13–10. But that was it for them.

Williams scored another TD on a 19-yard pass from Palmer. Malaefou MacKenzie caught a pass from Palmer for a 15-yard touchdown. Kileen

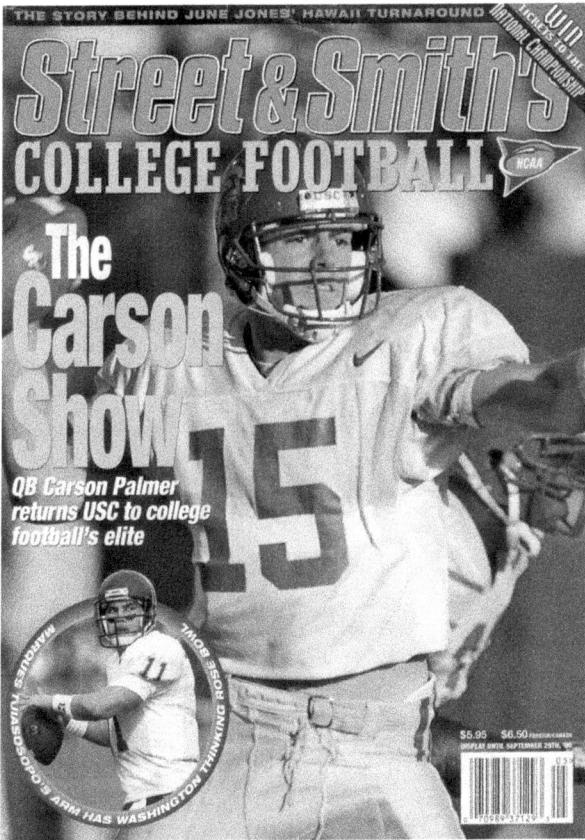

Carson Palmer, winner of the Heisman Trophy, passed for 425 yards and four touchdowns in the 44–13 dismantling of Notre Dame in 2002. *Sporting News Archives.*

kicked two more field goals of 27 and 29 yards, Sultan McCullough scored on an 11-yard run and MacKenzie once again scored, on a 10-yard pass from Palmer. USC was ranked fourth in the final poll, while ND made it to ninth.

## October 18, 2003:
## USC 45–ND 14 (Notre Dame), 80,795

Pete Carroll had arrived. The Trojans won twelve games, lost one to California, 35–31, and earned another national championship. Notre Dame had no chance as USC steamrolled into South Bend, winning 45–14. Notre Dame was 2-3, and USC had not lost a game. New quarterback Matt Leinert threw for 351 yards and four touchdowns. Keary Colbert started the scoring by taking an 18-yard pass for a TD from Leinert. The Irish came right back

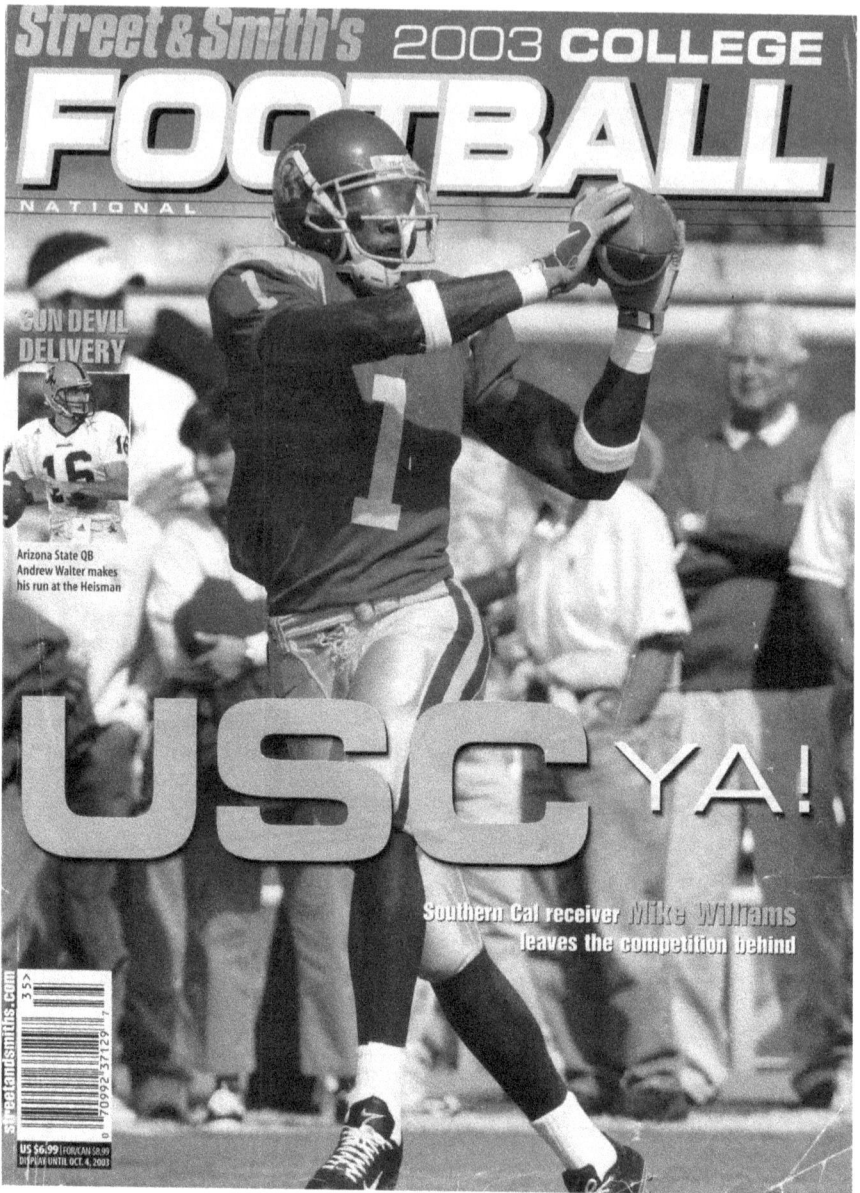

Wide receiver Mike Williams had a breakout season as a freshman in 2003 with eighty-one receptions for 1,265 yards and fourteen touchdowns, all USC freshman records. He helped the Trojans beat the Irish 45–14 in 2003 and 41–20 in 2004. *Sporting News Archives.*

as Julius Jones scored on a 22-yard run, Reggie Bush cruised 55 yards for a score and Anthony Fasano took a 2-yard pass from Brady Quinn for another touchdown. But it was all USC after that. Mike Williams scored on a 7-yard pass from Leinert, Hershel Dennis on a 3-yard pass and Gregg Guenther on a 7-yard pass from Leinert. A 29-yard field goal by Killeen and a 2-yard run by Dennis made the final score 45–14. Whew!

## November 27, 2004:
## USC 41–ND 10 (L.A. Coliseum), 92,611

The dominance of college football and of Notre Dame by USC continued in 2004. Carroll undressed Willingham, as the Irish coach, for the last time. The Trojans won thirteen straight games and looked like they would never get beat, and Carroll won his second national championship. Their only close game was a 31–28 victory over Stanford. Matt Leinert won the Heisman Trophy with an incredible year. His quarterback rating (156) was out of

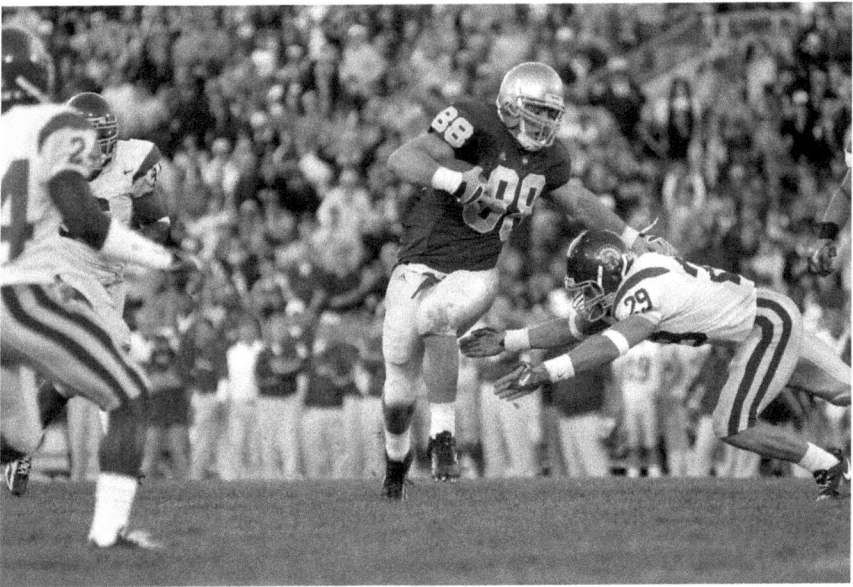

One of the greatest games in the series in 2005 reached a climax in a fourth-quarter drive led by Notre Dame's Brady Quinn, culminating in a 31–27 lead. But wait! There was too much time on the clock, and Matt Leinert threw a 51-yard pass to Dwayne Jarrett and a first down on the ND thirteen. USC scored to win, 34–31. *ND Archives*.

sight, and he completed 269 passes out of 412, with thirty-three touchdowns and only six interceptions!

Notre Dame, meanwhile, came to town under Willingham's tutelage (for the last time) with a 6-4 record, which was not terrible. Forget it. USC made Irish stew for the third year in a row, as Leinert passed for 400 yards and five touchdowns.

Notre Dame came out strong as Brady Quinn led the Irish on their longest drive of the season—92 yards—throwing a 1-yard pass to Billy Palmer. Ryan Killeen kicked a 39-yard field goal for USC, but D.J. Fitzpatrick answered with a 28-yarder for a 10–3 Irish lead. Well, that was their last fun of the night, as the Trojans outscored them, 38–0. Leinert capped an 80-yard drive by throwing a 12-yard TD pass to Dwayne Jarrett. Then he passed to Jarrett for a 54-yard touchdown. Killeen kicked a 42-yard field goal in the third quarter, as the Trojans took a 20–10 lead. Then Leinert followed with a 69-yard TD pass to Reggie Bush, a 35-yarder to Steve Smith and a 23-yard TD pass to Jason Mitchell to finish the scoring.

Quinn completed only fifteen of twenty-nine passes for 105 yards. Tyrone Willingham was history. Notre Dame went on to be blown out of the Insight Bowl by Oregon State, 38–21. It was the end of the great experiment. Notre Dame fired Willingham and went looking for a new coach.

# CHARLIE WEIS (0-5) VS. PETE CARROLL (5-0), 2005–2009

## October 15, 2005:
## USC 34–ND 31 (Notre Dame), 80,795

Now it was Charlie Weis's turn to be dismantled by the Big Cardinal and the Gold Machine—five straight years no less. The new coach for 2005, who had served as offensive coach for the Super Bowl–winning New England Patriots, seemed to be a wise choice when he won four of his first five games before meeting USC. He even broke out the legendary green jerseys that had brought Notre Dame to victory in 1977.

The 2005 USC game was one of the most competitive of the entire series. It seemed that USC was far superior, but master strategist Weis did the only thing

The Games

Many people regard Matt Leinert as the greatest of all USC quarterbacks because of his achieving a remarkable record (37-2) as a starter, guiding USC to national championships in 2003 and 2004 and winning the Heisman Trophy in 2004. He never lost to Notre Dame. *Sporting News Archives.*

possible to stay in the game—control the ball. The Irish did have the most success when they kept the ball out of the hands of Reggie Bush and Matt Leinert. They could only do it for so long, however, but they gave it a noble try.

Reggie Bush scored first on a 36-yard run, and Mario Danelo converted. But Travis Thomas answered with a 16-yard run and a conversion by D.J. Fitzpartrick. LenDale White came back with a three-run run and a Danelo conversion. But the second quarter was all Notre Dame's as Jeff Samardzija scored on a 32-yard pass from Brady Quinn, and Tom Zbikowski followed up with a 60-yard punt return, with Fitzpatrick converting after both TDs. So Notre Dame led at halftime, 21–14. Irish euphoria! For now.

The only scoring in the third was another TD by the unstoppable Bush on a 45-yard scamper, with Danelo kicking the extra point. The score was tied,

21–21. Then ND answered with a 32-yard field goal by Fitzpatrick. And Reggie Bush—yawn—came back once more to score on a 9-yard run, with Danelo converting, making it 28–24. Then Brady Quinn went to work with five minutes left. He marched ND down the field like he was Joe Montana. He finished off ND scoring with a 5-yard scamper himself. Fitzpatrick kicked, and it was 31–28. Heaven for the Irish!

But wait! There was 2:04 left. Time enough for Matt Leinert to drive the length of the field and score. The only problem is that he faced a fourth down and nine. What did he do? Nothing short of the spectacular. He completed a 61-yard pass to Jarrett that put USC on the ND 13. After a series of plays, USC was trying to score when the Irish nailed Leinert at the goal line. Game over! Irish win! Wait a minute! Leinert fumbled the ball out of bounds. The Trojans had time for one last play. They made it pay, with Leinert scoring with an assist from Bush. Final score was 34–31. This had to be one of the greatest games in the USC-ND history. Each team fought back like there was no tomorrow. There wasn't. Nobody deserved to lose. But one did.

What happened in Charlie's ensuing four years against USC is not worth mentioning, but I'll do it anyway. He lost 44–24, 38–0, 38–3 and 34–27. Did he give up? Probably not, but Notre Dame did. Goodbye, Charlie.

## November 25, 2006:
## USC 44–ND 24 (L.A. Coliseum), 91,800

Notre Dame had to come back, but it wasn't easy. It came into the 2006 game 10-1 and ready to kill. Charlie was hanging in there. USC, meanwhile, was going its merry way, 9-1, having lost only to Oregon State at Corvallis, 34–31. USC's John David Booty passed for 265 yards with three touchdowns, while Heisman candidate Brady Quinn didn't do badly, completing twenty-two of forty-five passes for 274 yards, three touchdowns and no interceptions. But USC jumped to a 14–0 lead and never looked back. Booty threw scoring passes to Jarrett of 9, 5 and 43 yards. Booty scored on a 1-yard sneak, Chauncey Washington on a 2-yard run and Brian Cushing on a 42-yard kickoff return. In the final analysis, USC at 11-2 finished fourth in the final polls, while the Irish at 10-3, who were killed their last two games, dropped all the way to seventeenth.

## October 20, 2007:
## USC 38–ND 0 (Notre Dame), 80,795

Charlie Weis did relatively great his first two years, although he lost in both the Fiesta and Sugar Bowls. But his next three years, he went a disastrous 3-9, 7-6 and 6-6. So long, Charlie.

Notre Dame came into the game in 2007 a ridiculous (for Notre Dame) 1-6, boasting one win over a terrible UCLA team. The Trojans, meanwhile, were 5-1, having lost only to Stanford, 24–23. The Irish should have stayed home, but they were already home. Mark Sanchez completed twenty-one of thirty-eight passes for 235 yards with four touchdowns and no interceptions. Wide receiver Vidal Hazelton scored from 48 yards out, tight end Fred Davis made a one-handed touchdown catch and freshman running back Joe McKnight raced 51 yards for his first touchdown. The USC defense allowed only 165 yards. The Irish ended up with one of their worst records ever, 3-9, while the Trojans finished 11-2 and No. 3 in the nation.

## November 29, 2008:
## USC 38–ND 3 (L.A. Coliseum), 90,689

Notre Dame made little improvement in 2008. It came in with a mediocre 6-5 record, while USC was up to its old tricks, having won nine games and losing only one to Oregon. Charlie Weis was in deep trouble, having to prove himself. He didn't. USC was ahead 31–0 before Notre Dame responded with its only field goal. The defense totally dominated the Irish, allowing 91 yards and four first downs. On offense, Mark Sanchez passed for 267 yards and two touchdowns. USC had one of its greatest seasons, ending 12-1, but ranked No. 2 behind Florida, which was 13-1. Notre Dame finished 7-6. Charlie started packing.

## October 7, 2009:
## USC 34–ND 27 (Notre Dame), 80,795

Poor USC. Pete Carroll had one of his worst seasons, finishing 9-4. Notre Dame, meanwhile, was an outstanding 3-1 (for Charlie, that is) when it faced off in South Bend. The Irish gave the Trojans a battle. USC scored first when wide receiver Damian Williams caught a 20-yard pass from Barkley.

Notre Dame answered with Robert Hughes scoring from two yards out. Then Jordan Congdon of USC kicked two field goals of 24 and 37 yards, so the first half ended 13–7 USC.

The Trojans scored first in the third when Williams took a 41-yard pass from Barkley. Then Notre Dame came back with Jimmy Clausen hitting Golden Tate for a 45-yard touchdown. Then Allen Bradford scored on a 3-yard run, followed by a 1-yard run by Joe McKnight for the Trojans. Notre Dame came back from a 34–14 deficit to score twice more—a 2-yard run by Clausen and a 15-yard pass to Tate from Clausen. Notre Dame beat Boston College and Washington State following the USC game, but then it finished the season with four straight losses to Navy, Pittsburgh, Connecticut and Stanford. Weis was fired Monday after the Stanford loss—so much for the ten-year contract extension that he signed in 2005; he settled for about $6.5 million. Poor Charlie.

Pete Carroll, on the other hand, was another case. After a phenomenal nine years, including a testimony that he would he never want to go anyplace else, Carroll announced his resignation on January 10, 2010. Five months later, the NCAA announced all the sanctions administered to the USC program. So much for loyalty and a job well done.

# BRIAN KELLY (1-1) VS. LANE KIFFIN (1-1), 2010–2011

## November 27, 2010:
## ND 20–USC 16 (L.A. Coliseum), 85,417

The 2010 season introduced new football coaches to Notre Dame and USC: Brian Kelly and Lane Kiflin, respectively. Notre Dame had not beaten USC since Pete Carroll's first year, so one had a feeling that it was due. USC went into the game 7-4, while the Irish were 6-5.

USC started off with a 3–0 lead when Joe Houston kicked a 45-yard field goal. But Notre Dame came back as Tommy Rees threw second-quarter 1-yard TD passes to Michael Floyd and Daryl Kuvara. David Ruffer missed the second extra point as the Irish took a 13–3 lead. In the third quarter, Houston kicked a 23-yard field goal, and Mustain, filling in for the injured

Matt Barkley, scored from 1 yard out. The score was tied, 13–13. But in the fourth quarter, Houston kicked a 37-yard field goal to put USC ahead, 16–13. But Notre Dame came back once more as Robert Hughes scored from 1 yard out.

Rees, making his third start, overcame four turnovers to throw two touchdown passes, and Floyd had eleven catches for 86 yards to pace the win. It helped Notre Dame that Ronald Johnson dropped a pass from Mustain at the Irish 15 with no ND defender in sight. The Irish also gave up a touchdown after going thirteen straight quarters without allowing one, the longest streak since 1980. USC beat UCLA the following week to finish 8-5, while the Irish defeated Miami in the Sun Bowl, 33–17, to also finish 8-5. Both coaches, while not satisfied, had decent starts. Neither finished in the top twenty.

## October 22, 2011:
## USC 31–ND 17 (Notre Dame), 80,795

Things got back to normal in 2011, as USC once more beat the Irish, 31–17. Notre Dame was 4-2 going into the game, having just won four in a row, including a 59–33 rout of Air Force the previous week. USC, meantime, was 5-1 and went on to finish 10-2 for the season and No. 6 in the final polls.

USC started off with a 17–0 lead before Notre Dame got on the board. Randall Telfer caught a 2-yard pass from Matt Barkley, and then Robert Woods had a 3-yarder from Barkley. Andrei Heidari kicked both extra points and followed them with a 25-yard field goal. The Irish hit the scoring column when George Atkinson returned a kickoff 96 yards for a TD. David Ruffer kicked the extra point. Minutes later, Ruffer kicked a 25-yard field goal, and the half ended, 17–10. In the third quarter, Jawanza Starling recovered a fumble on his own 15-yard line and rumbled 85 yards for the score. Heidari kicked the extra point. Notre Dame came back when Jonas Gray ran 25 yards, followed by Ruffer's kick, and the score was 24–17. Robert Woods finished the scoring on a 14-yard pass from Barkley, followed by Hedari's extra point, making it 31–17.

Well, USC is ranked No. 1 in many preseason polls for 2012, while Notre Dame is lurking in the shadows. If past years are any indication, one will undoubtedly be in for a few surprises. Two things are for sure: Kelly and Kiflin will be back—as of now.

PART II
# THE COACHES

## Wins and Losses

1. *Lou Holtz of ND (9-1-1)*

2. *Pete Carroll of USC (8-1)*

3. *Frank Leahy of ND (8-1-1)*

4. *John Robinson of USC (8-3-1)*

5. *John McKay of USC (8-6-2)*

6. *Howard Jones of USC (6-8-1)*

7. *Knute Rockne of ND (4-1)*

8. *Elmer Layden of ND 4-2-1*

9. *Joe Kuharich of ND (3-1)*

10. *Terry Brennan of ND (3-2)*

10. *Gerry Faust of ND (3-2)*

10. *Bob Davie of ND (3-2)*

13. *Ara Parseghian of ND (3-6-2)*

14. *Jess Hill of USC (2-4)*

15. *Hugh Devore of ND (1-0)*

16. *Lane Kiffin of USC (1-1)*

16. *Brian Kelly of ND (1-1)*

18. *Paul Hackett of USC (1-2)*

19. *Dan Devine of ND (1-5)*

20. *Jeff Cravath of USC (1-4-1)*

21. *Sam Barry of USC (0-1)*

22. *Don Clark of USC (0-3)*

22. *Hunk Anderson of ND (0-3)*

22. *Tyrone Willingham of ND (0-3)*

25. *Ted Tollner of USC (0-4)*

26. *Charlie Weis of ND (0-5)*

27. *Larry Smith of USC (0-6)*

# No. 1: Lou Holtz of Notre Dame (9-1-1), 1985–1996

Lou Holtz of Notre Dame is the only coach to have won nine games in this vaunted series. However, Pete Carroll, John Robinson and John McKay of USC and Frank Leahy of ND all are lurking behind with eight wins. The surprise is that Parseghian, one of the greatest coaches of all time, had a lousy 3-6-2 record against USC. The great Howard Jones of USC did not do so hot either at 6-7-1. In Holtz's tenure, ND was in the rut of winning eight games in a row—or was it that USC was in a rut of losing—before the Irish and Trojans tied one. Six coaches bear the burden of never having won a USC-ND game. That's a heavy burden.

Lou Holtz likes to tell a story about his high school football coach, Wade Watts, who told Lou's parents that he should go to college and become a football coach. Years later, Watts said, "I meant you should coach high school—not Notre Dame!"

But that's Holtz for you. A self-described pipsqueak who did not excel in either academics or sports became one of the most successful and recognizable football coaches in NCAA history. His secret? He never gave up. Never. That's probably why he is a success today even on ESPN as Dr. Lou, renowned football commentator.

Holtz in his autobiography *Wins, Losses and Lessons* said that he asked his team to follow three basic rules: do what is right, do your very best and treat others how you'd like to be treated. "These three rules are all you need, whether you are a coach, a player, a parent, a child, an employee, or an employer," he said.

Lou apparently was born to be a football coach. No matter where he coached, as a graduate assistant, as an assistant coach or as a head coach, he always had success. He started 0-11 at USC (that's the University of South Carolina), taking one year to turn the program around completely—not only going 8-4 but also beating Ohio State, 24–7, in the Outback Bowl!

Listen to what some of the people who know him best as a coach, husband and friend said about him in *Fighting Spirit* by Holtz and John Heisler.

Offensive guard Tim Grunhard said, "Coach Holtz is big in the emotional and psychological impact, but he is definitely not overbearing physically. But by caring and his motivation, we respect him very much."

Defensive end Flash Gordon said, "I think one of Coach's greatest assets is the way he motivates us."

# The Coaches

Linebacker West Pritchett said, "I think everybody really felt that the greatest thing Coach Holtz does is sell winning. He makes us believe in ourselves...At the same time, he'll be able to throw in a one-liner and keep everybody loose."

His wife, Beth, said, "Lou has been a lot of fun to be around...he makes people feel good to be around him."

Secretary Jan Blanzi said, "He's very much in control at all times. He's very much a perfectionist. He demands the best of others because he demands the best from himself."

Boyhood friend Frank Dawson said, "Lou Holtz is the same person I've known since back in the 1940s...My relationship with him is one of my treasured assets. My life would have been different if I didn't know him. What makes him different are his humility and his ability to ask questions."

Louis Leo Holtz was born on January 6, 1937, in Follansbee, West Virginia, a small steel mill town in the northern sliver of the state between Pennsylvania and Ohio. His family was very poor, and Lou started selling newspapers for six dollars per week when he was nine years old. He said that he was a poor student and a poor athlete because he was small, but he learned his life's mantra early: never give up. He said that he made his debut on the gridiron at the age of nine and played through high school and college, never weighing more than 165 pounds.

He said that he realized when he was nine years old that "the mental anguish you feel from letting down your coaches and teammates far exceeds any physical pain that might be inflicted on the football field...I might get pounded and squashed, but I would never quit." Lou added that he wasn't a very good athlete or a very mature student, but he had a "natural inclination to teach. I know my assignments on the football field, but I also knew everyone else's."

Eventually, he found his way to Kent State, where he was the lightest linebacker in college and also started his coaching career part time at a high school. This led to graduate assistant jobs and eventually to assistant coach positions at Iowa, William and Mary, Connecticut, South Carolina and Ohio State. He was hired as head coach at William and Mary (13-20) in 1969, which led to jobs at North Carolina State (33-12-3), Arkansas (60-21-2), Minnesota (10-12), Notre Dame (100-30-2) and, eventually, South Carolina (33-37). He married the love of his life, Beth Barcus, on July 22, 1961. They have four children: Skip, a former assistant and current coach of the University of South Florida; Luann; Kevin, who holds three Super Bowl rings from working in the Dallas front office; and Liz.

Lou Holtz's record against USC was 9-1-1. His closest game was his first year in 1986, 38–37, when Notre Dame had to rally from 18 points down and win on a John Carney field goal. *ND Archives.*

Lou won a national championship in 1988 and finished in the top twenty in the final polls nine out of his eleven years. But some of his favorite memories are the USC games. First of all, there was 1986, his first year, when Notre Dame had to come from being behind 37–20 in the fourth quarter to win on John Carney's 19-yard field goal. Also memorable was the 1988 victory, 27–10, which gave the Irish a national championship before 93,829 at the Coliseum.

In 1989, Notre Dame was ranked No. 1 with an 18-game winning streak going into the game at South Bend. The Trojans led, 17–7, at half, but the Irish bounced back to win, 28–24. The 1990 game was a nail-biter at the Coliseum, with the Irish edging the Trojans, 10–6. ND won only 24–20 in 1991, tied the Trojans 17–17 in 1994 and lost its only game to USC with

Holtz as coach in 1996, 27–20. His bowl record, an unremarkable 5-4, fits right in with the Irish's history of poor bowl showings.

Holtz retired from Notre Dame after the 1996 season. The supposition was that he was tired of battling the admissions office. He wanted great athletes who were great students or could become great students at Notre Dame, and he didn't always agree with the admissions office. He sheds no light on the matter in his autobiography, *Wins, Losses and Lessons*, other than it was "the right thing to do."

After that, he said, "Coaching again was the furthest thing from my mind. I figured that once you had been at Notre Dame, the only place left to go was heaven." He was looking forward to golfing, working in his garden, fishing, traveling with his wife and enjoying his grandchildren. His wife had survived throat cancer when Mike Magee, the athletic director at the University of South Carolina, called…and soon Lou was back in coaching.

"I was in my early sixties, and I still believed I had enough energy to go back and coach a few more years," Lou wrote in *Wins*. "There is a rule of life that you are either growing or dying…The minute we try to maintain, we start dying. When I left Notre Dame, I wasn't tired of coaching, I was tired of maintaining and I wasn't smart enough to know the difference."

Holtz stayed at South Carolina from 1999 to 2004, when he retired again, and at this writing, at the age of seventy-five, he is a football analyst for ESPN with no plans to return to coaching…yet.

# No. 2: Pete Carroll of USC (8-1-1), 2001–2009

Not counting Pete Carroll's first and last season, he went 82-9. 82-9! You're kidding me! That's crazy. That has to be one of the greatest runs in history. Howard Jones and Frank Leahy won a lot, but Carroll won eleven or twelve games seven years in a row. No one else has done that.

USC was on hard times when Athletic Director Mike Garrett had to "settle" for Pete Carroll in 2001 when no one else would take the job. Carroll, a veteran of the NFL, had no experience in college coaching or recruiting. Carroll was at a crossroads when he was offered the job at USC. He was considering various opportunities in business, but apparently that was too calm a life for him.

"I knew I had to be more active, more energized," he said in *Fight On!*, so he jumped at the USC opportunity. But many people, especially alumni, were vehemently opposed to the hiring. Some said that they would never support the school again until Carroll was tossed out. They soon changed their tune.

Peter Clay Carroll was born the son of James Edward and Rita Carroll in San Francisco. He was a good athlete as a youngster and attended Redwood High School in Larkspur, but he had trouble being allowed to go out for football as a freshman because he only weighed 110 pounds. "I think he put some rocks in his pocket," said Bob Troppmann, his coach at Redwood High, in *Fight On!* "There's no way they were going to keep him away from the football field." He made up his shortcomings by working harder than anyone else, and as a result he starred in baseball, football and basketball. In 1969, he was named the school's Athlete of the Year and was later inducted into the Redwood High School Hall of Fame.

Carroll attended College of Marin, a community college, where he lettered in football his second year before transferring to University of the Pacific. He played free safety and was honored by the Pacific Coast Athletic Conference both years. Carroll tried out for the World Football League and got a job in sales. Carroll then became a graduate assistant at Pacific. Strange as it may seem, he was then hired by the Arkansas coach—who happened to be Lou Holtz—to become an assistant working with the secondary. Carroll, impressing all of his head coaches, moved on to be an assistant at Iowa State and then Ohio State. Then he became defensive coordinator at North Carolina State, finally ending up as assistant head coach and offensive coordinator at the University of Pacific.

But in 1984, the NFL came calling, and he was named defensive coach of the Buffalo Bills. Then he spent five seasons with the Minnesota Vikings as defensive coach. In 1994, he was hired as head coach of the New York Jets, but they finished 6-10 and he was fired. In 1985, he was hired as defensive coach of the San Francisco 49ers and then head coach of the New England Patriots in 1997. His team won the division title the first year, but he failed to make the playoffs the next two years and was fired in 1999. He then was cornerbacks coach for the Seattle Seahawks before he was hired by USC.

Carroll's first year at USC was a disaster, as he finished 6-6, even losing to the University of Las Vegas in the Las Vegas Bowl. Things were to change quickly, and many wondered why considering his mediocrity in the pros.

In *Fight On!*, Bisheff and Schrader reported that *Boston Globe* columnist Bob Ryan, who followed Carroll's career, had an answer. "His problem was his personality. His failing is an essential decency and enthusiasm package that just doesn't have the same effect with guys drawing paychecks as it does with college players...I think it is nothing to be ashamed of...Is it more important to be remembered as an effective take-no-prisoners coach or as a tremendous human being who also happens to have a lot of football knowledge to impart?" After going 6-6, including the loss in the Las Vegas Bowl, Carroll's teams went off the charts. His records were 11-2 in 2002, 12-1 and a national championship in 2003, 13-0 and a national championship in 2004, 12-1 but losing No. 1 to Texas in the Rose Bowl in 2005, 11-2 and a Rose Bowl win in 2006, 11-2 and a Rose Bowl win in 2007, 12-1 and a Rose Bowl win in 2008 and 9-4 and an Emerald Bowl win in 2009.

Many people analyzed his success. "He's one of those people in a position of power that you respect, but they never have to ask for it," said USC all-American wide receiver Mike Williams. "If we had to go jump off a bridge, he could sell that to our team."

Wide receiver Keary Colbert echoed Williams in *Fight On!*: "He can get on you, but that's all out of love. He expects great things out of players. Guys do the right thing because they look up to Coach Carroll."

Carroll had his own reasons for his success: "I'm absolutely convinced that the only way you can do this is to be yourself. You don't have a chance to succeed if you try to be someone else."

"Pete Carroll instilled in us what we were playing for," said quarterback Carson Palmer in *Fight On!* "Looking back, he made us realize how hard we had to work to get to the top."

Carroll's teams finished in the top four nationally for seven consecutive years, he was named Coach of the Year by different groups and conferences for four straight years and the Trojans won thirty-four straight games. I think you could say that Pete Carroll made an impact on USC and college football.

And Carroll's record against Notre Dame was pretty incredible, even if it started off with a 27–16 loss. Quarterback Carlyle Holiday and running back Julius Jones led the Irish to a fairly easy victory. After that, it was all USC. It's definitely worth recounting. In 2002, quarterback Carson Palmer passed for 425 yards and four touchdowns. USC outgained the Irish 610 yards to 109 in a 44–13 rout. It was more of the same in 2004, as each team scored one more point in the Trojans' 45–14 win. This time, Matt Leinert passed for 357 yards and four touchdowns as Reggie Bush ran for 89 yards. The match in 2005 was undoubtedly one of the great games of all time. Irish quarterback Brady Quinn rallied ND to a 31–27 lead with just over two minutes remaining in the game. But Leinert united the troops and walked off with a devastating (to Notre Dame) 34–31 victory. But 2006 was back to business as usual when the Trojans polished off ND, 44–24. Dwayne Jarrett was again the hero as he caught three touchdown passes from quarterback John David Booty and made a one-hand catch to set up a fourth. The year 2007 was no better for the Irish. The Trojans rumbled to their greatest margin of victory, 38–0, before a South Bend crowd no less. Mark Sanchez, making his second straight start at quarterback, completed twenty-one of thirty-eight passes for 235 yards, with four touchdowns with no interceptions. In 2008, the Trojans again throttled the Irish, this time by a 38–3 score, and Carroll closed out his career with a 34–27 win at South Bend.

Off the field, Carroll was just as charismatic. He helped found A Better LA, a charity devoted to diminishing gang violence in Los Angeles. In 2009, he also started CampPete.com, an online game billed as a "ground-breaking Web site aimed at bringing Coach Carroll's unique Win Forever philosophy to kids all over the country."

Carroll and his wife, Glena, have two sons, Brennan and Nathan, who are both assistant coaches for the Seahawks, and a daughter, Jaimie, who played on the USC volleyball team.

After all of Carroll's great success, things began to fall apart. Why? Pete Carroll indicated that he got an offer he could not refuse. Just before the NCAA released a report on several major violations of the rules at USC, Carroll announced that he was taking the head coaching job with the Seattle Seahawks. Many people thought that this was a strange and major turnaround for someone who claimed that he dedicated his life to being a Trojan. USC was accused of several violations, but the main one was Reggie Bush accepting free housing accommodations for his parents. Carroll quickly denied that his leaving had anything to do with the NCAA sanctions. He said that he knew nothing about the alleged violations and took the job in Seattle because of the "extraordinary opportunity." His actions were not well received.

Columnist Bill Plashke wrote in the *Los Angeles Times* that Carroll went "from a coach who presided over the greatest days in USC football history to one who was in charge of its biggest embarrassment. He goes from saint to scallywag. Carroll says he didn't know about the Bush violations. That now seems impossible…he made $33 million from violations that will cost his old school its reputation, and folks here will never look at him the same."

Mike Florio of the *Sporting News* said that the Seahawks should fire Carroll: "Justice won't truly be served until the only coaching Carroll ever does entails holding an Xbox controller." Then in 2010, the Football Writers Association of America said that it would take back USC's Grantland Rice Trophy for 2004.

Carroll signed a five-year deal with Seattle in 2010 and completely renovated the Seahawks, only going 7-9 but becoming the first 7-9 team in

NFL history to win a division title. He even beat the New Orleans Saints but then lost to the Chicago Bears. Carroll repeated the same mark in 2011 and, as of this writing, is still there.

Only Carroll and maybe a few other players and coaches truly know what happened at USC. His career certainly can be examined with a jaundiced eye. But three things are certain: Pete Carroll won lot of games at USC, turned out some fine football players and gave USC fans many great moments.

# No. 3: Frank Leahy of Notre Dame (8-1-1), 1941–1953

Frank Leahy, the most famous Irishman who ever coached Notre Dame, was only a half a step behind Carroll, tying one game against USC and going 8-1-1. Leahy was one of the two greatest coaches who ever lived, both of whom coached at Notre Dame—Knute Rockne, who finished with a winning percentage of .881, and Leahy, who had "only" .864.

But Leahy was an enigma. Some people thought he was really strange. Others worshipped the ground he walked on. Two things, however, were certain: he was definitely a character to remember, and he was definitely a hell of a football coach.

"Frank Leahy was the most incredible man I ever met," noted Wells Twombley in his biography *Shake Down the Thunder!* "He added dignity and a new dimension to the expression 'fighting Irishman.' He had his faults. I make no attempt to portray him as a saint, faultless in every way. He was not. He was quite human. But he did practice what he preached…When the going got tough, Frank Leahy was tough enough to get going."

Francis William Leahy was born on August 27, 1908, in O'Neill, Nebraska, and moved with this parents and five brothers and sisters to Winner, South Dakota. Before he was in his teens, Frank was a working cowboy escorting cattle sometimes one hundred miles across the Badlands. He was attracted to sports and was allowed to go out for the high school football team when he was in the eighth grade because he weighed 155 pounds. He had success as a tackle at Winner High School and attended Notre Dame, where he played on the line for Knute Rockne from 1928 to 1931.

"Oooooooh, I tell you, it was love at first sight," Leahy said in the strange speech pattern that Twombley revealed in his biography. "I never felt so

Catholic in my life as the first time I saw that school." Rockne also loved him almost immediately.

"No matter what the rest of us did on the football field, Frank always made us seem like we weren't putting out," his friend and teammate Moon Mullins noted in *Shake Down the Thunder!* "He was such a perfectionist that it scared you. I think that's why Rockne loved him so much—and did you know Frank was just like him?"

When Leahy was injured, and Rockne took him to the Mayo Clinic in Minnesota, Frank confided to Knute that he wanted to be a football coach, and Rockne thought it was a wise decision. "I'm going to start working on getting you a job as soon as we get back to South Bend," Twombley reported. And he did, and Leahy was an assistant coach at Georgetown University, Michigan State and Fordham, where he coached the famous "seven blocks of granite," which included Vince Lombardi, the future coaching legend of the Green Bay Packers. In 1935, Leahy married his girlfriend, Floss, the former Florence Reilley, with whom he had eight children, and in 1939, he was named head coach at Boston College, where he stayed until Notre Dame came calling in 1941.

Leahy's eleven years at Notre Dame were nothing short of phenomenal. He went 8-0-1 his first year and was off and running, with winning years of 7-2-2, 9-1-0, 8-0-1, 9-0, 9-0-1 and 10-0 and national championships in 1943, 1946, 1947 and 1949.

USC, of course, was one of his major victims. His victories over USC included wins of 13–0, 26–6, 38–7, 32–0, 9–0 and 48–14. The year 1941 had one of the closest games, even though the Trojans lost six games that year. Their failure again to make extra points cost them the game. USC lost in 1942, 13–0, and there were no games again until 1946 because of the war. The late '40s were dominated by the Irish until 1948. A tie by USC in the last game of the year cost the Irish a record four straight national championships. The Trojans were an unremarkable 6-3 when they met Notre Dame at the L.A. Coliseum in the last game of the year. "The three touchdown underdogs outcharged, outfought and nearly outscored the South Bend Supermen," Cameron Applegate noted in *The Game Is On*. This time, the Trojans made their extra points, and Notre Dame had to score with thirty-four seconds left just to tie the game.

Leahy also coached four Heisman Trophy winners—Angelo Bertelli in 1943, Johnny Lujack in 1947, Leon Hart in 1949 and Johnny Lattner in 1953—and he even recruited Paul Hornung, winner in 1956. He also coached thirty-six all-Americans, thirteen of them being consensus. His teams went undefeated in thirty-nine straight games and were unbeaten in six of the eleven years he coached at Notre Dame. Eleven of his players are in the National Football Foundation's Hall of Fame.

In 1949, the legendary Red Grange said that Leahy was one of the greatest coaches ever: "Leahy gets more out of his material than other coaches... Look at the succession of outstanding quarterbacks Frank has had. That isn't an accident; it's the result of hard work...Frank is a perfectionist—his players seldom make a mistake."

Jack Connor, a former player and brother of all-time Notre Dame great George Connor, described what other players thought of Leahy in his book *Leahy's Lads*. "He was a phenomenal individual," said former player and coach Bernie Crimmins. "He was a hard-nosed guy who expected you to give far beyond what you thought you had."

"Leahy was the greatest coach in the history of the game," said center Jerry Groom and captain of the 1950 team. "The sad thing about Leahy is that people will never know what a really great guy Frank was...he absolutely loved his players...he would do anything for any one of them, and he didn't care if they were on the seventh string."

"I only played for two coaches in college and pro ball," said all-American quarterback Johnny Lujack, "Frank Leahy and George Halas. I think Leahy was ten times better than Halas."

"To me," former quarterback great Frank Tripucka said, "Leahy was so much smarter than other coaches. As far as the basics and fine points of the T-formation, everything came from Leahy."

Twombley pointed out that Leahy's players and coaches did not really get to know him personally on the field but did off the field. His way of showing disapproval on the field was through sarcasm: "Oh, Joseph Slignaigo, you missed that block. Do you really want to play for the University of Notre Dame? Let's run that play over again and see if Joseph wants to protect his teammate." He loved to refer to his players by their full name, and he loved even more any player who loved football as much as he did and worked as hard as he did.

"Leahy's biggest fault was his inability to relax and enjoy life," Twombley wrote. "He was a worrier and a pessimist...It was his all-consuming devotion to football that eventually drove him from the game he loved and devoted his life to."

The consensus of his fate seems to rest on two things: Leahy's deteriorating health and the fact that the new and great president Father Theodore Hesburgh did not like Notre Dame being known as a football factory and wanted a change. "They forced him to resign," Frank Leahy Jr. said in *Shake*

No greater duo than Coach Frank Leahy (1941–53) and Athletic Director Moose Krause (right) ever walked across Notre Dame's hallowed campus or led its memorable football teams. *ND Archives.*

*Down the Thunder!* "He's never admitted it and neither will Hesburgh, but that's what happened." But he will never be forgotten. Leahy died on June 21, 1973, at age sixty-five in Portland, Oregon, of congestive heart failure.

# No. 4: John Robinson of USC (8-3-1), 1976–1982, 1993–1997

John Robinson not only was a Notre Dame killer, he was also one of the Trojans' most successful football coaches. His record of 104-35-4 stands 1 percentage point behind John McKay's, but his record against Notre Dame only stands second to Pete Carroll at 8-3-1. In his first tenure with USC (1976–82), Robinson lost in 1977 but never lost again after that. His biggest victory came in 1978, when a 27–25 come-from-behind victory gave the Trojans a national championship.

Robinson, who was a surprise selection as USC coach, proved to be popular with the fans, alumni and the media. He was almost the second coming of John McKay.

Born in Chicago on July 25, 1935, Robinson was raised in Daly City, California, where he grew up with future Hall of Famer John Madden. After playing sports in high school, he attended the University of Oregon, where he played end. Sensing his interest in coaching, Oregon coach Len Casanova hired Robinson as an assistant, a position he retained for eleven years. After becoming an assistant under John McKay, a fellow Duck, in 1972, he coached for the Oakland Raiders before being named top man at USC in 1976. Everyone was shocked by the choice. McKay assistants Marv Goux and Dave Levy were lobbying for the job.

In *Fight On!*, Robinson claimed that USC chancellor John Hubbard called him from an airport in Washington, D.C., and asked him if he wanted the job. "They flew me down to introduce me," Robinson said, "and you could tell it was a shock to everyone. All those coaches on the staff thought they had a chance. [Dave] Levy would have been as good as anyone." Levy became an assistant athletic director, and Goux stayed on Robinson's staff.

But Robinson's first game was a disaster, getting killed by Missouri, 46–25. "I thought our team was ready," Robinson said in *Fight On!* "Maybe we overprepared. We made some colossal mistakes in that game. It was ugly." Not for long. The Trojans righted the ship and went 11-0, including a 17–13 victory over Notre Dame and a Rose Bowl victory over Michigan, and Robinson endeared himself to the fans and alumni. His sojourn was helped by a continuing stream of great tailbacks—Ricky Bell, Charles White and Marcus Allen—and no one would ever forget the hard-hitting Ronnie Lott in the secondary.

Notre Dame had a bit of revival in 1977, winning 49–19, but the Trojans came back in 1978 to ensure their national championship with a come-from-behind victory over Notre Dame. Late in the third quarter, USC led by three touchdowns.

"Then came Joe," Travers reported in *USC Trojans*. "If you were there you saw Montana wake up the echoes and single-handedly silence the home crowd. He was everything he would be against Dallas or Cincinnati or Denver [in the pros]. He was the best I ever saw." But quarterback Paul McDonald rallied USC and drove the team downfield so that Frank Jordan could kick a game-winning field goal, 27–25, with two seconds on the clock. That was enough to propel them to a national championship.

"He [Robinson] was very passionate, and he loved USC," McDonald said in *USC Trojans*. "The only time I ever talked to Robinson was on game day,

John Robinson went 105-35-4 as head coach of USC, almost the equal of John McKay, but he only won one national championship (1978) compared to McKay's four. He also did very well against the Irish at 8-2-1. *From the* Daily Breeze.

during TV timeouts. He was good at that. He'd pull you aside, put his arm on your shoulder, and try to lighten the moment. He always made sure you realized there was a fun aspect to the game."

But in 1969, tailback Charles White went them one better by rushing for 261 yards in forty-four carries to help win the Notre Dame game, 42–23. Robinson himself had fond memories of epic battles with Notre Dame. He was unusually late going to meet the press after one of the games. "I'm sorry," he said. "But I wanted to stay out there and listen to the band and soak up all the atmosphere and everything. This is such a special place, and you never know when you will be back again. This is what college football is all about."

Robinson had good years through 1982, but all of a sudden he was gone. He said he needed a change. He went back to pro football, where he lasted eight years with the Los Angeles Rams before returning to USC again. This time he didn't fare as well, going 2-2-1 against Notre Dame, and then he was gone again. Things just didn't work out, he said. In *Fight On!*, he said, "Sometimes things don't always go your way. Coaching can be like that. And when that happens, you become vulnerable. It is part of the business." In 2010, he was helping coach defense for San Marcos High School.

Robinson had some memorable years and great teams at USC and will always be remembered.

# No. 5: John McKay of USC (8-6-2), 1960–1975

It is probably safe to say that John McKay was the most popular coach that USC ever had. He went 127-40-8, but strangely enough he was only 8-6-2 against Notre Dame. However, McKay won four national championships, in 1962, 1967, 1972 and 1974. His best wins over the Irish came in 1962 (25–0), which helped him win his first national championship; in 1964 (20–17), knocking Notre Dame out of the national championship; in 1972 (45–23); and in 1974 (55–24), known for Anthony Davis running wild.

"John McKay wasn't just a football coach," Bisheff and Schrader said in *Fight On!* "He was equal parts strategist and comedian. He was the football equivalent of Johnny Carson, as quick with a quip as he was drawing up a new play. He could be brilliant and moody, funny and quick-tempered, cocky and yet, somehow, surprisingly insecure. His players feared him, his assistants worshipped him, and the fans and the media loved him."

"At home he was a twenty-four-hour-a-day football guy," said Pat Haden, quarterback in 1973 and 1974. (Haden was the best friend of son J.K. McKay and lived with the McKays his senior year in high school.) "He was very smart, very right. He did like westerns, either movies or novels. As a coach he was very tough, especially on game day. He loved steak sandwiches and vodka and liked to play golf. Most of all, he loved the university." He had a unbelievable facility to finding the right position for a player. "I think he was the best evaluator of talent that I have ever seen," Haden said.

McKay was as remarkable on the field as off it. "I thought that was God up there watching me," said Manfred Moore, who played for him from 1971 to 1973, in *Fight On!* "That's why I went at full speed all the time."

Dick Beam was another assistant who loved to work for McKay. "I've never been around a guy who had a wit like him. I've also never been around a guy

John McKay, arguably the greatest Trojan coach of them all, finished 8-6-2 against Notre Dame and 127-40-8 for his career at USC. *USC Archives.*

who knew as much football...I learned more football in one year than I had in my entire life. He knew how to diagnose teams and how to take them apart."

John Harvey McKay was born on July 5, 1923, in Everettville, West Virginia, to Scotch-Irish parents, John and Gertrude. His father, a mine superintendent, died of pneumonia when John was thirteen, and he was raised in Shinnston, Virginia, with four brothers and sisters. He was an all-state running back and a star guard on the basketball team in Shinnston High School and received a football scholarship to Wake Forest. He returned home after a year to work as a electrician's assistant in a coal mine before joining the air force in 1942 and serving as a tail gunner on B-29s in the Pacific.

After the war, he entered Purdue University in 1946 but shortly transferred to the University of Oregon, where he played halfback in the same backfield with Norm Van Brocklin, future Los Angeles Rams great. After he graduated, Oregon coach Len Casanova hired him as an assistant coach, and he stayed there for eleven seasons. In 1959, he joined the USC staff and was named head coach in 1960 when Don Clark resigned.

McKay got off to a slow start, losing to Notre Dame in 1960, 17–0, and in 1961, 30–0. He did not endear himself to the USC faithful. They sang a different tune in 1962 when McKay won his first national championship and throttled the Irish, 25–0, along the way. Notre Dame got revenge in 1963, 17–14. But the Trojans made up for it in 1964 coming from 17 points down to beat the Irish. Other great wins came in 1962, 25–0; 1967, 24–7; 1972, 45–23; and the incredible come-from-behind win over the Irish in 1974, 55–24.

He coached so many great players that it is almost impossible to count: quarterbacks Pat Haden, Pete Beathard, Craig Fertig and Jimmy Jones; running backs O.J. Simpson, Mike Garrett, Anthony Davis, Sam Cunningham and Ricky Bell; offensive tackles Ron Yary, Pete Adams and John Vella; flanker Lynn Swann; guard Damon Bame; ends Hal Bedsole, Marvin Powell, Ron Drake and Sam Dickerson; defensive backs Nate Shaw and Dennis Thurmond; linebackers Adrian Young and Richad Wood; and defensive ends Jimmy Gunn and Charles Young.

McKay left USC after the 1975 season, to go to the new NFL team the Tampa Bay Bucs, for "more money and new challenges." He will be missed by the Trojan faithful forever. McKay died on June 1, 2001, of complications resulting from diabetes. He was seventy-seven.

# No. 6: Howard Jones of USC (6-8-1), 1931–1940

Howard Jones, one of the greatest coaches in USC history, suffered the same fate as the great Ara Parseghian of the Irish. Neither had a good record against his favorite opponent. Jones, whose career boasted a great record of 121-36-3, had a 6-7-1 record against the Irish. He seemed to beat everyone else regularly, but not Notre Dame. He ended up with three national championships as a player at Yale, one as a coach at Yale and four as the coach of USC. Not bad.

Jones, who was born in Excello, Ohio, in 1885, played for Yale in 1905–7 and was named all-American twice. After graduating, he coached Syracuse to a 6-3-1 season before coaching at Yale, Ohio State and Iowa, where he beat Knute Rockne's Notre Dame team, 10–7, in 1921. After coaching Duke a year, he was named head coach of Southern Cal following the recommendation of Rockne. He soon proved to be one of the best.

"He was the toughest taskmaster I ever knew," said Nick Pappas, a tailback who played for Jones from 1935 to 1937. "Jones was the kind of guy who would tell you to run through a wall—and you'd ask him, how high. If you weren't ready when he called, boy, you'd never be ready. There was never a tougher man who ever put out a football team in my estimation. He didn't know what pain meant."

"He was a great man," said lineman Gene Clarke. "He taught me to suck in my stomach and hold out my chest. He taught me things to carry along in life. He taught me to play it clean—we didn't know how to play dirty."

Jones won four national championships, five Rose Bowl games and eight Pacific Coast Conference titles. After probably his biggest victory, a come-from-behind win at Notre Dame in 1931, the normally staid Jones ran on the field and kissed the first player he saw, center Stan Williamson. Never flamboyant like Rockne or Stagg, Jones was just known as the perfect coach.

"His teams had more straight power than deception," said guard Nate Barragar, captain of the 1929 team. "He always believed that if the men did their individual jobs, the play should go...We'd actually tell the other team where we were going to run the ball—and then just ran it through that spot."

"It was a darn good blocking team," said Al Wesson, longtime USC sports publicist. "He was the first to introduce cross-blocking where two of his players would block one guy on the other team to open a hole for his runners."

When he swore at half-time at a California game, everyone nearly fell in a faint, recalled lineman Gene Clarke. "He would hardly glance at a boy coming off the field after playing his heart out," Wesson said. "But when the game was over, in the privacy of the training quarters, he'd hunt out every boy who had played, thank him for what he had done, and be sure that any injuries, no matter how trivial, were immediately cared for."

Jones, who was born in 1885 (three years before Rock) in Ohio, played three seasons at Yale University, 1905–7, and Yale won the national championship each year, going an unbelievable 28-0-2. He became head coach at Syracuse University in 1908 (compiling a 6-3-1 record) before returning to Yale as head coach. Incredibly, he coached one year there, going 10-0 and winning another national championship. (The year was marked by a 15–0 victory over Syracuse, coached by his brother, Tad.)

Jones became head coach at Ohio State, where he finished 6-1-3. Jones then went into private business before returning to coach Yale in 1913 to a 5-2-3 record. Greener pastures called, and he went to Iowa, where he had a 42-17-1 record, with a perfect 7-0 season in 1921, including a 10–7 win over Rockne and Notre Dame. In 1924, he went to Duke, where he finished

4-5 before moving on to USC, where he became one of the greatest coaches in school history. All in all, Jones, while a great coach, was reported to be a complete opposite of Rock. Where Rockne was a great speaker and a natural showman, Jones was said to be stern and humorless. It didn't stop him from being one of the greatest coaches who ever lived.

But Jones did not have an easy time with the Irish. He finished 6-9-1 in his sixteen years there, but he certainly started off strong, winning the national championship in 1928, 1931 and 1932. He died of a heart attack at his home in Toluca Lake, California, in 1941. He was inducted into the College Football Hall of Fame in 1951.

# No. 7: Knute Rockne (4-1), 1926–1930

Knute Rockne still remains *the* coach of all American college football. It is true that he reigned when the sport was just starting, but other coaches of the time also had a chance to be No. 1. They weren't. It was Rockne. It was a combination of his personality, his character and his football knowledge that seemed to set him above everyone else. He still has the highest winning percentage in football history, .881, with a 105-12-5 record.

It would be easy to dismiss the Rock as the product of another era. How could his players compete with the mind-blowing athletes of today? Well, I don't know how, but they could. Rockne had that special something that made his players want to go out and kill for him to win. There has never been another like him.

Knute Rockne was born Knut Larsen Rokne in Norway in 1888, the son of a blacksmith and wagon maker. He immigrated to Chicago with his parents when he was five years old. He played football and ran track in high school, and after graduating, he worked four years at the Chicago Post Office. He saved his money and at twenty-two headed to Notre Dame, where he was an outstanding student and all-American football end in 1913. He and quarterback Gus Dorais helped the Irish to defeat a powerhouse Army team, 35–13, in 1913, a game said to be the first major contest where the forward pass was a primary move. He was a laboratory assistant in chemistry until he was offered the head coaching job at Notre Dame in 1918.

In his thirteen years as head coach before being killed in a plane crash in 1931 at age forty-three, he had five undefeated seasons, three national

# Notre Dame vs. USC

Knute Rockne, owner of the highest winning percentage of major college football coaches, was 4-1 against the USC Trojans before being killed in a plane crash in March 1931 at age forty-three. *ND Archives.*

championships and a record of 105-12-5, the best record of all time for a major college. (In fact, Frank Leahy, one of his predecessors, is second with a .864 mark, which includes his stint at Boston College.)

Rockne, of course, was one of those who started the Irish's long love affair with the University of Southern California in 1926. There are two versions of how the series started, as I said earlier. One is that USC athletic director Gwyn Wilson and his wife went to Nebraska to see Notre Dame play the Huskers in the hope of finding a national rival. The real story, however, seems to come from author Murray Sperber in his book *Shake Down the Thunder.* Sperber reported that ND and USC officials met as early as December 1925 to decide on a home-and-home series that would benefit both schools. Sperber also noted that when Rockne refused grandiose offers from USC to become head coach, he highly recommended Howard Jones, whom he coached against when Jones was at Iowa, for the job. Needless to say, the rest is history. Jones became one of USC's greatest coaches, going 121-36-13 in sixteen years at the helm for a not-so-shabby .750.

# No. 8: Elmer Layden (4-2-1), 1934–1940

Elmer Layden, one of the legendary Four Horsemen, started his Irish coaching career against a tough Texas team coached by Jack Chevigny, a former ND player who had something to prove. Layden ended up losing, 7–6. But in the next game against Purdue, the Irish fared better, winning 18–7. Layden went on to finish 6-3 his first year, including his first victory over USC, 14–0. His players included such early Irish greats as end Wayne Millner, center John Robinson, quarterbacks William Shakespeare and Andy Puplis, halfbacks Benny Sheridan and Mike Layden, guards Joe Kuharich and Jim McGoldrick and fullback Mario Tonelli.

Layden basically went on winning six to eight out of nine games every year. He did very well against USC, winning his first two games in 1933 and 1934. They kissed their sisters in 1936, and the Irish won again in 1937, 13–6, before USC won the next two and lost the last.

Layden's best year was in 1938, when they went 8-1, losing only to USC, 13–0. But Notre Dame still ended up No. 5 for the season in the final poll, and USC No. 7. The Irish were 7-1-1 in 1934 and 7-2 in 1939 and 1940. Not bad.

Elmer Francis Layden was a consummate gentleman as a football player, a coach, a college athletics administrator and a professional sports executive. He was born in Davenport, Iowa, on May 4, 1903. He played sports at Davenport High School before attending the University of Notre Dame. He was a member of what is often referred to as the best backfield in college history, and he was all-American fullback in 1924.

Elmer Layden, one of the fabled Four Horsemen, also coached Notre Dame from 1934 to 1940, finishing 4-2-1 against the Trojans and 47-13-3 overall. *Collegiate Collection.*

He played one year of professional football before becoming head football coach at Columba College in Dubuque, Iowa. He finished 8-5-2 after two seasons and then took the head coaching job at Duquesne in Pittsburgh from 1927 to 1933; there he compiled a 48-16-6 mark. After that, he went to Notre Dame, where he was head coach through 1940, compiling a record of 47-13-3. Then he was commissioner of the National Football League before he resigned in 1946 to go into business in Chicago.

Layden's "commitment to Catholicism, his activity as a layman, his speaking ability, his smooth public demeanor, his spotless private life and his general intelligence" helped him get the job as Notre Dame coach, according to Murray Sperber in *Shake Down the Thunder*. "Layden's smooth wit and diplomatic demeanor concealed a very tough and ambitious personality." He especially had Rockne's hard-nosed, pragmatic attitude.

In the spring of 1940, the Notre Dame administration reduced the football squad to 60 players from 115. The new administration did not like the emphasis on football. Also, the new administrators only offered Layden a one-year extension, and Layden chose "more money, more security and a better life for my family" by going to the NFL as commissioner at $20,000 per year. Enter Frank Leahy. Layden died on June 30, 1973, at age seventy in Chicago.

# No. 9: Joe Kuharich (3-1), 1959–1962

It's kind of funny that the worst coach in Notre Dame history (.425 and 17-23) ranks this high. But he won three games and lost only one against USC. In reality, Kuharich wasn't that bad actually. His wins included 19–6 and 13–7 over Oklahoma, 17–0 and 30–0 over USC, 43–22 over Pittsburgh and 35–12 over Iowa.

Kuharich was born on April 14, 1917, appropriately in South Bend, Indiana. He played guard for Layden from 1935 to 1937, and Layden called him one of the best and smartest players he ever coached. Kuharich began his coaching career as an assistant at Notre Dame in 1938 and then coached at the Vincentian Institute in Albany, New York, before playing for the Chicago Cardinals in 1940 and 1941. After going into the military, he returned to the Cardinals in 1945, his last year as a pro. Then he coached for the Pittsburgh Steelers and the University of San Francisco and became

Coach Joe
Kuharich (right),
with Terry
Brennan (left)
and quarterback
George Izo
in 1959, did
not have a
remarkable
career at Notre
Dame, but his
record against
the Trojans was
almost perfect at
3-1. *Sporting News
Archives.*

head coach of the Chicago Cardinals in 1952 and then of the Washington Redskins before returning to Notre Dame.

It seemed that Kuharich never adjusted to college football and appeared satisfied to finish 5-5 every year. Of course, the alumni did not like this attitude, and Notre Dame and Kuharich parted ways, both seemingly happy about it, and he became supervisor of NFL officials.

But his teams beat USC in 1959, 16–6; in 1960, 17–0; and in 1961, 30–0, losing in 1962, 25–0. He didn't lack for some great players—quarterbacks Daryl Lamonica and George Izo, halfback Bob Scarpitto, guard Nick Buoniconti, tackle Joe Carollo, fullback Joe Perkowski and ends Jack Snow and Monty Stickles. But when it was his time to leave, he returned to the NFL. Kuharich died on January 25, 1981, in Philadelphia. He was sixty-three.

NOTRE DAME VS. USC

# No. 10: Terry Brennan of Notre Dame (3-2), 1954–1958

Terry Brennan was a speedy halfback who played for Frank Leahy from 1945 to 1948. I remember when he was named coach of Notre Dame. He seemed a perfect choice. He was good-looking, Irish, Catholic, smart and personable. What else could one want? Well, maybe someone who was a little older. Terry took over the team at the ripe age of twenty-five and finished five years later with a record of 32-18, certainly not up to Notre Dame standards since Knute had lost twelve games in thirteen years and Leahy eleven in eleven years. But he still gave it a noble effort.

In his first year, he finished 9-1, with only a loss to Purdue. USC was dispatched with aplomb, 23–17, and Irish eyes were still smiling as ND was ranked fourth in the nation. Not bad for his first year. And he only went down slightly his second year, finishing 8-2 in the polls (USC finished seventeenth and thirteenth those same years). Terry only lost to Michigan State and a big one to USC, 42–20. He, of course, had Paul Hornung for three years but not a whole lot else.

His biggest win came on November 16, 1957, when the Irish stopped the Oklahoma juggernaut in its tracks, as well as its forty-seven-game winning streak. The Irish scored in the fourth quarter with four minutes to go when Bobby Williams faked to Nick Pietrosante up the middle and pitched out to Dick Lynch, who scored from the 3-yard line.

Frank Leahy opened a hornets' nest in 1956 when he criticized Terry, saying that the team quit cold in a 48–8 loss to Iowa. It didn't help that they had already lost six games before they faced the Hawkeyes and then also lost, 28–20, to USC and finished 2-8, the worst season in Notre Dame history. It seems like it only takes one bad season to turn the tide of opinion.

Brennan, who was born on June 11, 1928, in Milwaukee, was a multisport star at Marquette University High School. He went on to Notre Dame, where the teams he played on from 1946 to 1948 did not lose one game. He then coached at Mount Carmel High School in Chicago and won three successful city championships before moving to Notre Dame in 1953 as the freshman football coach. He took over from Leahy the following year at twenty-five years old. He wasn't too used to losing.

After Brennan was summarily dismissed the end of the 1958 season, he worked as conditioning coach for the Cincinnati Reds in spring training in 1959 and then hung up his jock. He worked in the financial world in Chicago and is still alive as of this writing with six children, twenty-five grandchildren and seven great-grandchildren. I would say that he successfully served and survived Notre Dame.

# No. 10: Gerry Faust of Notre Dame (3-2), 1981–1984

It would be easy to say that hiring Gerry Faust was the second-biggest coaching blunder that Notre Dame ever made. After all, his winning percentage of .535 (30-26-1) ranks just ahead of Kuharich. But looking at other hires of recent years, many have not been too swift, and it's not such an easy decision to make. After all, Faust went 3-2 against USC. He actually went 5-6, 6-4-1, 7-5, 7-5 and 5-6 in his five years. It's not the worst record of all time, but Irish fans and alumni were used to winning a lot. And he had some big wins. In his very first game, he beat LSU, 27–9. Against USC, he lost the first two games and won the next three. He couldn't have been a slouch at recruiting, bringing such storied names into the Irish lair as linebackers Bob Crable and West Pritchard, tight end Mark Bavaro, defensive ends Mike Gann and Andy Heck, flankers Tim Brown and Mark Green, running back Allen Pinkett and defensive back Dave Duerson.

Gerard Anthony Faust was born on May 21, 1935, in Dayton, Ohio, and was a three-year letterman at quarterback for the University of Dayton. In 1962, he became coach of Moeller High School in Cincinnati, where he compiled a record of 178-23-2 and four national high school championships. As a feeder school to Notre Dame, Faust was enamored of the school, and it with him. So when Dan Devine retired, Faust became head coach. After five years at Notre Dame, he became head coach at the University of Akron, where he stayed for nine seasons, compiling a record of 43-53-3. He retired after the 1994 season and today is a motivational speaker headquartered in Fairlawn, Ohio.

# No. 10: Bob Davie (3-2), 1997–2001

The handsome and personable Bob Davie seemed to be a good choice as Notre Dame football coach. But after five seasons of mediocrity—by Notre Dame standards—Davie was told to go his way, and Stanford coach Tyrone

Willingham was hired, becoming the first black Irish head coach. Davie, an assistant coach for twenty years, had good seasons (9-3) in 1998 and 2000, but each time the Irish lost a bowl game. Against USC, Davie fared well, winning three games in a row (25–24, 38–21 and 27–16). Davie also attracted lot of great recruits, like quarterback Carlyle Holiday, running backs Julius Jones and Ryan Grant, wide receiver David Givens, linebackers Rocky Boiman and Mike Goolsby, center Jeff Faine and cornerbacks Vontez Duff and Shane Walton, many regulars ion the NFL.

Robert Edward Davie Jr. was born on September 20, 1954, in Sewickley, Pennsylvania. He was a sports star in high school in baseball, football and basketball. He accepted a football scholarship to the University of Arizona but grew homesick and returned to Pennsylvania, enrolling at Youngstown University, where he was starting tight end for three years. Following graduation, he took a job as a graduate assistant at the University of Pittsburgh. This was followed by assistant coaching jobs at Arizona, Pittsburgh, Tulane and Texas A&M. He came to Notre Dame as a defensive coordinator under Lou Holtz, was quite successful and was named head coach when Lou retired.

Davie, who was an ESPN color analyst, accepted the job as head coach of the University of New Mexico for 2012.

# No. 13: Ara Parseghian of Notre Dame (3-6-2), 1964–1974

Ara Parseghian seems to be one of those guys who was born to be a football coach. His .836 winning percentage at Notre Dame was third to Rockne and Layden, but he may have even more accomplished. The teams—and the schedules—were probably a lot tougher in the 1960s and early 1970s, and Ara's record was never worse than 7-2-1 (twice). And the Irish played everyone who was anyone, especially USC, Michigan, Miami, Michigan State, Oklahoma, LSU, Texas and Alabama. He won three major bowls, usually when he wasn't expected to. He was 39-6-1 at Miami of Ohio. He didn't do great at Northwestern (nobody has), but at 36-35-1 it probably was great for a non-football school.

Parseghian was born Ara Raoul on May 21, 1923, of an educated multilingual Armenian and a fearless French mother. His father, Michael, had fled Turkey at age sixteen on a Greek ship to Athens on which he spent two years as an accountant. He managed to reach Akron, which had a large Armenian population, and was subsequently drafted and sent to France to be liaison between French and American officers. He met a French woman who subsequently introduced him to a French girl named Amelia. They met, married and had three children: Gerard, Isabella and Ara. The second son soon began playing football in junior and senior high school in Akron before serving in the navy two years during World War II and later attending University of Miami at Ohio, where he played football for three years. He was drafted in the thirteenth round in 1947 and played a year for the Cleveland Browns before an injury ended his playing career. He became freshman team coach in 1950 at Miami under Coach Woody Hayes. When Hayes left to go to Ohio State, Parseghian was named head coach. After five successful years at Miami, he spent eight years at Northwestern, becoming coach at Notre Dame from 1964 to 1974.

Probably the main reason he left coaching was because of a serious disease running through his family, Niemann-Pick Type C, a neurological disorder. He has lost his three youngest grandchildren at ages nine, ten and sixteen to the disease, and he created the Ara Parseghian Medical Research Foundation to help combat it. Parseghian's success has gone far beyond the gridiron, but he would be the first one to admit that football paved the way.

"The first time I ever saw Ara Raoul Parseghian (as a basketball player at Miami), I knew there was something special about him," wrote Tom Pagna, his close friend, assistant coach and author of *Notre Dame's Era of Ara*. He constantly proved this at Notre Dame and following his retirement.

There were three defining moments of Ara's era. The first came in 1964. Ara took virtually the same team with which Hugh Devore earned a 2-7 record in 1963 and almost made them national champs. Notre Dame had rolled into the L.A. Coliseum with a 9-0 record, having allowed 47 points. And they took a 17–0 lead at halftime to make the season perfect—up to then.

Assistant Coach Tom Pagna reported that it was Parseghian's decisions and leadership that made the Irish victorious. In 1964, he converted running backs Pete Duranko, Paul Costa and Jim Snowden to the defensive line. Jack Snow was converted from halfback to split end, and quarterback John Huarte was brought off the bench to win the Heisman Trophy. Ara turned some of the players like Bill Wolski, Nick Eddy, Kevin Hardy, Alan Page, Jim Lynch, Jim Carroll, Tony Carey, Tom Longo and Nick Rassas into all-Americans and others into some of the finest players to ever suit up for Notre

Coach Ara Parseghian and quarterback Terry Hanratty made a great team at Notre Dame for three years, 1966–68. The Irish record in that period was a not-so-shabby 24-4-2. *ND Archives.*

Dame. The second half of 1964 wrecked their aspirations, but it didn't stop Parseghian from being named the Coach of the Year and setting the tone for the next decade.

The second moment came in 1966. The famous game between Michigan State and ND that ended in a 10–10 tie brought Ara bad publicity for playing for a tie. He ended that in short order when ND massacred USC the following Saturday, 51–0, and were named national champs.

The third came in 1977. Finally, Notre Dame had a perfect season with a 38–10 dismantling of Texas in the Cotton Bowl that gave them the national championship.

"Winning attitudes, work attitudes, enthusiasm and perfectionism were all generated by Ara's personality," Pagna said in his book. "The 1964 team learned there was strength in this pride. It was the very thing that would give them an edge and exactly what had been missing before Ara arrived. It was not so much the blocking and tackling he taught them but rather the inner strength that would catapult mediocrity into greatness."

Today, Ara is eighty-nine years old and is still advocating enthusiasm and perfectionism.

# No. 14: Jess Hill of USC (2-4), 1951–1956

Jess Hill, a former college athlete and professional baseball player, was USC football coach from 1951 through 1956 but was best known as athletic director from 1957 to 1972. He might have been the best athlete of all the coaches listed here. As the head football coach, he only won two of six from the Irish, but he was 45-17-1 for his six years. In 1952, USC finished 10-2 and beat Wisconsin, 7–0, in the Rose Bowl. In 1954, he finished 8-4 and lost to Ohio State in the Rose Bowl, 20–7. In 1956, USC finished 8-2 but was banned from a bowl game. Hill beat Notre Dame his last two years, 28–20 and 40–12.

Jesse Terrell Hill was born in Yates, Missouri, and moved to Corona, California, as a boy. He attended Corona High School and Riverside Junior College before transferring to USC, where he earned letters in football, track and baseball. He was a running back on the 1928 USC national championship team and averaged 8.2 yards per carry as a senior for a Trojan team that won the Rose Bowl in 1930. As a junior in 1928, he won the NCAA broad jump title with a jump of 25 feet, ⅞ inch.

He played professional baseball before joining the navy in World War II. In 1946, he was hired to coach freshman football and track at USC. He was head track coach in 1949–50, and his teams won national titles. After his stint from 1951 to 1956 as USC football coach, he became athletic director until 1972. Jess Hill died on August 31, 1993, a USC legend.

Jess Hill's record (1951–56) at USC was 45-17-1, but he finished 2-4 against Notre Dame. *USC Athletic News.*

# NO. 15: HUGH DEVORE OF NOTRE DAME (1-0), 1963

Hughie Devore was an institution at Notre Dame and apparently a very likable one. He filled in as football coach in 1945 during the war years, and the team went 7-2-1 and again in 1963 as an interim to Ara, but he was less successful then at 2-7. His one crowning glory is to be the only Notre Dame coach to go undefeated against USC at 1-0. His team won, 17–14, in 1963.

Devore was born on November 25, 1910, in Newark, New Jersey, where he was a three-sport star in high school. He played right end at Notre Dame from 1931 to 1933. After graduation, he stayed one year at Notre Dame as freshman football coach before joining Jim Crowley at Fordham in 1935. Except for one year to help out Notre Dame in 1945, he served as coach at Providence, Holy Cross, St. Bonaventure and New York University. In 1953, he went to the NFL's Green Bay Packers before going to Dayton and the Philadelphia Eagles. The likable Devore, not known as the world's best football coach but as "Hughie," always helped Notre Dame when it needed him. He also served as an assistant athletic director from 1964 to 1966. He died on December 8, 1992.

# NO. 16: LANE KIFFIN (1-1), 2010–2011

Lane Kiffin, thirty-seven, has been coaching college football since 1999 and comes from a football family. His dad, Monte Kiffin, a longtime defensive coordinator in the NFL, is now USC's defensive coordinator. Kiffin did not set the house afire in 2010, but he did finish 8-5, which included a loss to Notre Dame, 20–16, but a win over UCLA, 28–14. He had big wins over Washington State, 50–16, and California, 48–14. In 2011, his offensive pyrotechnics continued as he had a great 10-2 record that included a 31–17 win over Notre Dame and a 50–0 cakewalk over UCLA. (That should be worth a contract extension itself.)

Born Lane Monte Kiffin on March 8, 1975, in Bloomington, Minnesota, after high school Kiffin served as a backup quarterback at Fresno State until he gave up his senior year to become a student assistant at FresNo. He was a graduate assistant at Colorado State University in 1999 before becoming a quality control assistant for the Jacksonville Jaguars. Pete Carroll hired him as tight ends coach at USC in 2001. Kiffin helped USC to a 23-3 record during his tenure. Al Davis of the Oakland Raiders hired him in 2007, making him the youngest head coach in NFL history at thirty-one. Following a 5-15 season, Kiffin was dismissed with some animosity by Davis and soon became the head coach at the University of Tennessee. He compiled a 7-6 record in 2009 and came to USC as head coach in 2010. Whew! That guy has been busy.

Kiffin apparently has a knack for staying in the news. Not only are the Trojans No. 1 in many preseason polls for the 2012–13 season, Silas Redd, premier Penn State running back, has also announced he is transferring there. Ah, college football.

# No. 16: Brian Kelly of Notre Dame (1-1), 2010–2011

*May the road rise up to meet you.*
*May the wind be always at your back.*
*May the sun shine warm upon your face;*
*the rains fall soft upon your fields.*
*And until we meet again,*
*may God hold you in the palm of his hand.*
*—traditional Irish blessing*

Ah yes, me laddie. The Irish are looking for greater blessings in 2012. Brian Kelly, the coach with the greatest Irish surname since Terry Brennan, hopes to put the "Fighting" back into the Irish for 2012. It's not going to be easy. Even the Notre Dame faithful and media seemed to be hoping for a seven- or eight-win season at best. The quarterback job hasn't been settled, and premier players—like six-foot-six tight end Tyler Eifert and linebacker Manti Te'o—seemed to be at a premium indeed. Time will tell.

The year 2010 didn't look too bad. Kelly ended 8-5 with a rare Irish bowl win over Miami, 33–17, and an even rarer victory over the Trojans, 20–16. The year 2011 also ended 8-5 but with a disheartening bowl loss to Florida State, 18–14. But after losing the first two games, the Irish won eight out of nine, including a 59–33 win over Air Force and a 56–14 win over Navy, a big deal since they had lost two in a row to the Middies. Unfortunately, USC

NOTE DAME VS. USC

took it to them again, 31–17, at South Bend. I don't know. The flesh may be willing, but the spirit seems to be weak.

Born Brian Keith Kelly in Everett, Massachusetts, into a Catholic family, Kelly had a father who was a Boston politician and had a start as a four-year letterman as linebacker at Assumption College in Worcester, Massachusetts. After graduation, he served as linebackers coach, defensive coordinator and softball coach at Assumption from 1983 to 1986. He then spent seventeen years at Grand Valley State as an assistant and head coach in Muskegon, Michigan, where he had a record of 118-35-2. This was followed by three years at Central Michigan and three at Cincinnati, where he had records of 19-16 and 34-6, respectfully. His success at Cincinnati seemed to be reason he was hired by Notre Dame in 2010 to replace Charlie Weis. The jury is out yet for Kelly, but a "return to glory" seems shaky at best.

# No. 18: Paul Hackett (1-2), 1998–2000

Mediocrity thy name has to be Paul Hackett. I hate to be brutally honest, but his record says it all: 32-38-1 and 1-2 against Notre Dame. He lost all the way around. After Robinson was history, Mike Garrett had trouble finding a coach. Even Lou Holtz was a candidate, but he turned USC down. Finally, they settled on Hackett, whom nobody was really crazy about. He did okay his first year. He started out with three wins, including one over Purdue and Drew Brees, but then he lost four games and ended up beating Notre Dame, 10–0, for his only victory against the Irish. Then they played in the Sun Bowl and lost to TCU. It was only downhill from there.

The Trojans went 6-6 in 1999, losing 25–24 to the Irish in South Bend. And in 2000, they were 5-7, losing once more to Notre Dame, 38–21.

Paul Hackett was born in Burlington, Vermont, and played football at Cal State Davis. After graduating, he was assistant coach of the freshman football team and then head freshman coach before becoming an assistant at the University of California at Berkley. After four years there, he worked in various coaching capacities for USC, the Cleveland Browns, the San Francisco 49ers, the Dallas Cowboys, the University of Pittsburgh and the Kansas City Chiefs before returning to USC as head coach in 1998. He most recently was quarterbacks coach for the Oakland Raiders.

# No. 19: Dan Devine of Notre Dame (1-5), 1975–1980

Unfortunately for Dan Devine, even if he won a national title in 1977 with Joe Montana, he never was really accepted by the Notre Dame faithful, especially the alumni. Even on the day of the 1977 game between ND and USC, "Dump Devine" stickers were being sold. He finished 53-16-1 at Notre Dame, but the fans always seemed to want more. In six years, he went 8-3, 9-3, 11-1, 9-3, 7-4 and 9-2-1. Not exactly bad. He also won three bowl games, only losing one. The real blot on his record was beating the Trojans only once, 49–19 (the famous green jersey game), in 1977. Anyway, my contention is that Devine was a great coach. His record (173-56-9) proves it.

Daniel John Devine was born in Augusta, Wisconsin, on December 22, 1924, and became a sports star at Proctor High School in Proctor, Minnesota. He enrolled at the University of Minnesota–Duluth, where he was captain of both the baseball and football teams. After a stint in the U.S. Army Air Corps in World War II, he became head high school football coach in Michigan before going to Michigan State as an assistant. He then served a few years at

The years 1976–78 featured another dynamic duo in Coach Dan Devine and Joe Montana, probably the most exciting college quarterback and the greatest pro quarterback of all time. *ND Archives.*

Arizona State before becoming head coach at the University of Missouri for twelve years, going a great 93-37-4. He went to the NFL's Green Bay Packers from 1971 to 1974 before being hired at Notre Dame to replace Ara.

In his later years, he served as fundraiser for Arizona State University, before returning to the University of Missouri as athletic director. He was elected to the College Football Hall of fame in 1985. Devine died on May 9, 2002, at age seventy-seven.

# No. 20: Jeff Cravath of USC (1-5-1), 1942–1950

Jeff Cravath, a center on the 1924–26 USC teams and also team captain, became head football coach in 1942 when Sam Barry went into the navy during World War II. Cravath was a good coach and led the team to a serviceable 54-28-8 record. Unfortunately, he only won one game against Notre Dame, 9–7, in 1950. Cravath did not do too badly. He finished 8-2 in 1943, and USC beat Washington in the Rose Bowl, 29–0. The Trojans didn't lose in 1944, finishing 8-0-2. In 1945, USC was 7-4 and lost to Alabama in the Rose Bowl, 11–2. In 1947, USC finished 7-2 but lost big in the Rose Bowl to Michigan, 49–0. The year 1948 was okay as they finished 6-3-1. That was the best he could do.

Newell "Jeff" Cravath was born on February 3, 1903, in Breckinridge, Colorado. His mother died at childbirth, and his father when he was six, and he was raised by his maternal grandparents. He played football at Santa Ana High School and then attended USC, where he also played on the football team. Upon graduation, he became a USC assistant under Howard Jones in 1927. He served as head coach at Denver University from 1929 to 1931. He returned to USC as assistant coach from 1933 to 1940. He did have a record of 8-3-1 against UCLA. After leaving football, he was a racing official at Santa Anita Park before becoming a rancher in El Centro, California. Cravath died at fifty of injuries he received in a traffic accident.

Jim Hardy, a 1942 quarterback for Cravath and later general manager of the Los Angeles Coliseum, said, "I would go to Cravath for advice where I would not even have gone to my family. He was a friend of all his players and a good coach. He was subjected to unreasonable pressure in his last year at USC, but he never lost his interest in the game and his deep attachment to the men who played for him."

## No. 21: Sam Barry (0-1), 1941

Sam Barry, a legend at USC, was head baseball and basketball coach and became head football coach at USC in 1941 as an interim between Howard Jones and Jeff Cravath. When he entered the navy, Cravath took over. Barry finished 2-6-1, but the games were generally close, except for a blowout to Ohio State, 33–0. He also lost only 20–18 to ND, and he tied the dreaded UCLA, 7–7. When Angelo Bertelli completed thirteen of twenty passes for the Irish in 1941, Sam proclaimed that "it was the greatest show of passing talent I've sever seen from anyone." Remember, it was still early for the passing game.

Justin McCarthy "Sam" Barry was born on September 17, 1892, in Aberdeen, South Dakota. He starred in baseball, basketball and football in high school in Madison, Wisconsin, before receiving his degree at University of Wisconsin–Madison. He started his coaching career at Madison High School before going to Knox College in Illinois, where he served as athletic director and head coach of football, baseball, basketball and track. When USC was in need of a new basketball coach, old colleague Howard Jones recommended him and the Barry-USC connection was born. Barry had unprecedented success in both baseball and basketball at USC. He actually did well his one football season considering the depleted talent. His team almost beat fourth-ranked Notre Dame and did beat Rose Bowl–bound Oregon State.

"His successes as a basketball, baseball and football coach would fill several books but it can be safely said that when Sam died suddenly…he left not one enemy along the trail of his phenomenal career…In the years to come, Sam Barry will be talked about in the same breath with Dr. Naismith when the development and progress of the game of basketball are discussed," wrote Paul Zimmerman in the September 25, 1950 edition of the *Los Angeles Times*.

## No. 22: Don Clark of USC (0-3), 1957–1959

Don Clark obviously will not go down as one of USC's all-time great coaches. In fact, not only was his record 13-16-1, he also lost all three games to Notre Dame and two to UCLA, with one tie. However, he did have his moment of fame in 1959 when the team started 8-0 and ended up losing only to UCLA and Notre Dame, believe it or not.

Born Donald Rex Clark on December 22, 1923, in Shurdan, Iowa, his family moved to Los Angeles when he was fifteen, and he played football at USC in 1942 before spending three years in World War II and returning to USC for his final two years, 1946–47. He was an assistant coach at the Naval Academy before he returned to USC and coached under Jess Hill. Then players recommended that he be named the next head coach. He was replaced in 1960 by John McKay, and Don retired to the family business in California. He died at age sixty-five after suffering a heart attack while jogging.

# No. 22: Hunk Anderson of Notre Dame (0-3), 1931–1933

Hunk Anderson's most famous football moments have to be when he was an all-American guard for Knute Rockne from 1919 to 1921. He was five-foot-eleven, 170 pounds, and Rock said that he was as tough and fierce a competitor as he ever had. The word was that the only guy in college football who matched him was Hall of Fame tackle Duke Slater, who weighed 220. Anyway, Rock's record when Hunk was there was 29-1. Not too shabby. Hunk was a likely successor for Rock and went 6-2-1 his first year (ranked third in the country), 7-2 his second year (ranked fourth) and 3-5-1 his last year. Unfortunately, USC had some of its best teams, and he lost to them every year, 16–14, 13–0 and 19–0. So much for leprechauns.

Heartley Hunk Anderson was born on September 22, 1898, in Calumet, Michigan, and attended Calumet High School before playing football for Rock at Notre Dame. He played football in the NFL for Cleveland and Chicago and was on the 1920s All-Decade Team. He coached the Detroit Lions in 1939 and also served as assistant coach at St. Louis University and North Carolina State. From 1942 to 1945, he coached the Chicago Bears, earning a record of 24-12. Hunk died on April 24, 1978, in Palm Beach, Florida, still bleeding Irish blue and gold.

# No. 22: Tyrone Willingham (0-3), 2002–2004

Notre Dame seemed to be really proud of naming its first African American football coach. It's too bad he only lasted three years, but unfortunately Ty, never known as Mr. Personality, never delivered. He looked better on paper than in the field. His three head coaching jobs resulted in a 44-36-1 at Stanford, 21-15 a Notre Dame and an embarrassing 11-37 at the University of Washington, the worst record in its 111-year history.

Poor Tyrone did not fare any better against USC. He lost the first game, 44–13, the second game, 45–14, and the third game, 41–10. Geez! Spare us the details.

Tyrone Willingham was born on December 30, 1953, in Kinston, North Carolina. He attended Jacksonville High School, where he lettered in football, baseball and basketball. He went to Michigan State University, where he played football and baseball and graduated in 1977. He was assistant football coach at Michigan State, Central Michigan, North Carolina State, Rice and Stanford before moving up to head coach. Willingham retired after his debacle in Washington, seemingly a nice, dedicated guy who was out of his element.

# No. 25: Ted Tollner of USC (0-4), 1983–1986

It seemed that Ted Tollner suffered a similar fate at USC. After the winning and personable McKay and Robinson, Tollner was never embraced by the USC faithful. Tollner's job wasn't easy since he immediately faced some NCAA sanctions. Unfortunately, he went 4-6-1, 9-3, 6-6 and 7-5, nothing to write home about. Also he had to face Notre Dame four times, and USC came away losers four times: 27–6, 19–7, 37–3 and 38–37. His one good year was 1984, when they finished 9-3 and beat Ohio State, 18–6, in the Rose Bowl. That held off the wolves for a while.

Ted Alfred Tollner was born on May 29, 1940. He was a quarterback on the 1960 California Polytech team whose plane crashed in Ohio, killing sixteen players, a manager and a booster. Tollner had exchanged seats with a player who was not feeling well. The player died in the crash, and Tollner survived, always wondering why.

He started coaching at Woodside High in California in 1963. He later coached at College of San Mateo, San Diego State and Brigham Young before serving as an assistant under John Robinson. After USC, he returned to San Diego State, where he coached seven more years. He spent a few more years in the NFL and is now retired.

# No. 26. Charlie Weis of Notre Dame (0-5), 2005-2009

In 2005, Charlie Weis, the rotund offensive coordinator from the New England Patriots, became another potential savior of the Notre Dame football program. He had some good years, but it was never to be. The important thing is that college football will never again see the days of Rockne, Jones, Leahy, Parseghian, McKay and Holtz. All the great high school players don't just go to USC, Notre Dame, Michigan, Ohio State and Texas any more. A top player could end up anywhere—even Boise State or Connecticut, for Pete's sake. That's not to say the coaching legends mentioned would not succeed today. They would always succeed; it's just that today they might find it a little more difficult.

Take Charlie! No, you take him, the Notre Dame faithful said. Well, the savior started out pretty good, going 9-3 his first year and then 10-3; it was all uphill after that. The downfall was 2007 when he finished 3-9, while the following 7-6 and 6-6 seasons did nothing to endear him to Irish hearts.

Weis's venture with the Trojans was sad indeed, except for 2005. That was the game where Matt Leinert of USC scored in the last second to send Brady Quinn and the Irish to a 34–31 defeat in one of the greatest games of the century. (There are a lot of them.) Both teams were great on offense, with the defense being a little suspect. Weis probably did his finest coaching job, keeping the ball out of the Trojans' hands until the last few minutes, when it was too late to come back. The next three years were disastrous as USC won 41–9, 38–0 and 38–3. In the last game, the Irish fought back, losing 34–27.

Charles Joseph Weis was born on March 30, 1956, in Trenton, New Jersey. He played football in high school but never in college, attending the University of Notre Dame. After graduation, he spent five years coaching high school football in New Jersey before going to South Carolina. He returned to New Jersey as the head coach of Franklin High School, where he made some connections with the New York Giants NFL team. Bill Parcells hired him as an assistant for offense and special teams—nobody explains how he got so lucky. In 1993, he became tight ends coach for the New England Patriots. From 1997 to 1999, he served as offensive coordinator of the New York Jets, who finished fourth in offense in the league. Bill Belichick hired him, and he served as offensive coordinator for the New England Patriots from 2000 to 2004, helping the Patriots win three Super Bowl titles.

That was enough for Notre Dame. When it could not get Urban Meyer, who went to Florida, the Irish settled for Charlie. He survived five years before he was fired and went to the Kansas City Chiefs as offensive coordinator, then to the University of Florida and finally to the University of Kansas as head coach for the 2012 season. It will be interesting to see what Charlie does next. Hopefully, Kansas does not have USC on its schedule.

# No. 27: Larry Smith of USC (0-6), 1987–1992

It probably is not totally fair, but USC and Larry Smith end up last because he had the poor luck to face Lou Holtz, who was on a roll against USC, six times. But Larry was a good coach who ended up 44-25-3 in his six years but also lost six games to the Irish. He never stood much of a chance. The scores were 26–15, 27–10, 28–24, 10–6, 24–20 and 31–23. Overall, Larry wasn't bad. He was 8-4, 10-2, 9-2-1, 8-4-1, 3-8 and 6-5-1. The last straw, of course, was losing a bowl game to Fresno State, 24–7.

Larry Smith was born in Van Wert, Ohio, on September 12, 1939, and was a three-sport star in high school. He played football at Bowling Green University, eventually earning a master's degree in education. First, he was a high school coach, and then he joined Bo Schembeckler at Miami University as defensive end coach. He spent four years as defensive coach with the University of Michigan. He was head coach at Tulane and Arizona before USC. His overall college coaching record is 143-126-7. Later, he worked as a commentator for Arizona football. He was diagnosed with leukemia in 1999 and died on January 28, 2008, at the age of sixty-eight.

# HEISMAN TROPHY WINNERS

## NOTRE DAME

Angelo Bertelli, QB, 1943
Johnny Lujack, QB, 1947
Leon Hart, end, 1949
John Lattner, RB, 1953
Paul Hornung, QB, 1956
John Huarte, QB, 1964
Tim Brown, WR, 1987

## USC

Mike Garrett, RB, 1965
O.J. Simpson, RB, 1968
Charles White, RB, 1969
Marcus Allen, RB, 1981
Carson Palmer, QB, 2002
Matt Leinert, QB, 2004

# FIFTY OF NOTRE DAME'S GREATEST PLAYERS

Gus Dorais, QB, 1913
Knute Rockne, end, 1913
George Glipp, RB, 1920
Jim Crowley, HB, 1924
Elmer Layden, FB, 1924
Don Miller, HB, 1924
Harry Stuhldreher, RB, 1924
Marchy Schwartz, HB, 1930
Wayne Millner, end, 1932
Chuck Sweeney, end, 1937
Bob Dove, end, 1941
Angelo Bertelli, QB, 1943
Creighton Miller, HB, 1943
George Connor, OL, 1947
Bill Fischer, OL, 1947
Johnny Lujack, QB, 1947
Leon Hart, end, 1949
Jerry Groom, OL, 1950
Ralph Guglielmi, QB, 1954
Paul Hornung, QB, 1956
Monty Stickles, TE, 1958
John Huarte, QB, 1964
Nick Rassas, DB, 1965

Nick Eddy, RB, 1966
Jim Lynch, LB, 1966
Steve Niehaus, OL, 1966
Alan Page, DE, 1966
Tom Schoen, DB, 1967
George Kunz, OL, 1968
Larry DiNardo, G, 1970
Dave Casper, TE, 1973
Gerry DiNardo, G, 1974
Luther Bradley, DB, 1977
Joe Montana, QB, 1977
Bob Golic, LB, 1978
Vegas Ferguson, RB, 1979
Bob Crable, LB, 1980
John Scully, OL, 1980
Tim Brown, WR, 1987
Frank Stams, LB, 1988
Todd Lyght, DB, 1989
Rocket Ismail, WR, 1990
Michael Stonebreaker, LB, 1990
Chris Zorich, DL, 1990
Jerome Bettis, RB, 1993
Tim Ruddy, OL, 1993
Bobby Taylor, DB, 1994
Shane Walton, DB, 2002
Brady Quinn, QB, 2005
Jeff Smardzija, WR, 2005

# FIFTY OF USC'S GREATEST PLAYERS

Mort Kaer, QB, 1926
Morley Drury, QB, 1927
John Baker, OL, 1929
Tay Brown, OL, 1930
Ernie Smith, DL, 1931
Aaron Rosenbrg, DL, 1932
Cotton Warburton, QB, 1932
Harry Smith, DL, 1937
Frank Gifford, HB, 1950
Des Koch, P, 1951
Jon Arnett, RB, 1955
Ron Mix, OL, 1957
Ernie Pinckert, RB, 1957
Marlin McKeever, DL, 1958
Mike McKeever, DL, 1958
Hal Bedsole, TE, 1963
Mike Garrett, RB, 1963
Tim Rossovich, OL, 1967
Ron Yary, OL, 1967
O.J. Simpson, RB, 1968
Sam Cunningham, FB, 1970
Jimmy Jones, QB, 1970
Lynn Swann, WR, 1973

Anthony Davis, RB, 1974
Pat Haden, QB, 1974
John McKay Jr., WR, 1974
Richard Wood, LB, 1974
Ricky Bell, RB, 1975
Marvin Powell, OL, 1976
Dennis Thurman, DB, 1977
Brad Budde, OL, 1979
Charles White, RB, 1979
Ronnie Lott, DB, 1980
Dennis Smith, DB, 1980
Marcus Allen, RB, 1981
Bruce Mathews, OL, 1982
Steve Jordan, PK, 1984
Jack Del Rio, LB, 1984
Tim McDonald, DB, 1986
Mark Carrier, DB, 1989
Leroy Holt, FB, 1989
Tim Ryan, DL, 1989
Junior Seau, LB, 1989
Johnnie Morton, WR, 1993
Tony Boselli, OL, 1994
Keyshawn Johnson, WR, 1995
Chris Claibourne, LB, 1998
Carson Palmer, QB, 2002
Matt Leinert, QB, 2005
Clay Matthews, LB, 2008

# BIBLIOGRAPHY

## BOOKS

Applegate, Cameron. *Notre Dame vs. USC: The Game Is On.* Hollywood, CA: Fiske/Milne, 1977.

Bisheff, Steve, and Loel Schrader. *Fight On! The Colorful Story of USC Football.* Nashville, TN: Cumberland House, 2006.

Brondfield, Jerry. *Rockne.* New York: Random House, 1976.

Connor, Jack. *Leahy's Lads.* South Bend, IN: Diamond, 1997.

Dent, Jim. *Resurrection: The Miracle Season that Saved Notre Dame.* New York: Thomas Dunne Books, 2009.

Garner, Joe. *Echoes of Notre Dame Football.* Naperville, IL: Sourcebooks, 2001.

Heisler, John. *"Then Ara Said to Joe...": The Best Notre Dame Football Stories Ever Told.* Chicago, IL: Triumph, 2007.

Holtz, Lou. *Wins, Losses and Lessons.* New York: William Moirrow, 2006.

Holtz, Lou, with John Heisler. *The Fighting Spirit.* New York: Pocket Books, 1989.

Hornung, Paul. *Golden Boy.* New York: Simon & Schuster. 2004.

Pagna, Tom, with Bob Best. *Notre Dame's Era of Ara.* South Bend, IN: Hardwood, 1976.

Rappoport, Ken. *The Trojans: A Story of Southern California Football.* Huntsville, AL: Strode, 1974.

Singular, Stephen. *Notre Dame's Greatest Coaches*. New York: Pocket Books, 1993.

Sperber, Murray. *Shake Down the Thunder: The Creation of Notre Dame Football*. New York: Henry Holt and Company, 1993.

Travers, Steven. *USC Trojans*. Lanham, MD: Taylor, 2006.

Twombley, Wells. *Shake Down the Thunder! The Official Biography of Notre Dame's Frank Leahy*. Radnor, PA: Chilton Book Company, 1974.

*2008 Notre Dame Football Guide*. Notre Dame, IN: Ave Maria Press, 2008.

*2003 Notre Dame Football Guide*. Notre Dame, IN: Ave Maria Press, 2003.

Wharton, David. *USC Football Yesterday and Today*. Lincolnwood, IL: West Side, 2009.

# REFERENCE WEBSITES

sports-reference.com.
und.com.
usc.trojans.
wikipedia.org.

# ABOUT THE AUTHOR

Donald James Lechman, a native of Colorado, worked as a reporter, critic and editor for the newspaper industry from 1960 to 2005. A graduate of the University of Colorado in journalism and a dedicated Buff, his columns appear regularly in the *Daily Breeze* newspaper in Torrance, California. You can also read him at donlechman.blogspot. com. His first book for The History Press, *Los Angeles Dodgers Pitchers: Seven Decades of Diamond Dominance*, is available through Amazon or at The History Press website. Besides being a devoted fan of baseball, football and basketball, he enjoys writing, reading, traveling with his wife, playing the guitar, watching movies, listening to music (especially Frank Sinatra and Ella Fitzgerald), playing basketball, going to the theater and concerts, working out and spending time with his two grandchildren. He teaches writing at Los Angeles Harbor College in Wilmington, has been married to artist Pat for thirty-eight years and has two adult children, Laura Ann and David Michael.

Visit us at
www.historypress.net

www.ingramcontent.com/pod-product-compliance
Lightning Source LLC
Chambersburg PA
CBHW060804100426

42813CB00004B/935